ST. FRANCIS
OF ASSISI AND THE
CONVERSION
OF THE
MUSLIMS

"Neither is there salvation in any other. For there is no other name under heaven given to men, whereby we must be saved." —Acts 4:12

ST. FRANCIS

OF ASSISI AND THE

CONVERSION

OF THE

MUSLIMS

WITH A CONCISE BIOGRAPHY OF THE SAINT

Frank M. Rega

*"Go ye into the whole world, and
preach the gospel to every creature. He
that believeth and is baptized, shall
be saved: but he that believeth not
shall be condemned."*—Mark 16:15-16

TAN Books
Charlotte, North Carolina

ISBN: 978-0-89555-858-9

Cover Illustration: St. Francis of Assisi preaching to the birds/St. Francis of Assisi preaching to the Mamluk Sultan Al-Kamil, by Bonaventura Berlinghieri (1235-1274), from 20 stories of the life of St. Francis, S. Croce, Florence, Italy. Photo Credit: Scala/Art Resource, NY.

Cover design by Milo Persic.

Printed and bound in the United States of America.

TAN Books
Charlotte, North Carolina

2011

Dedication

To all the admirers and followers of the great Saint of Assisi, who either found Jesus Christ or were drawn closer to Him because of the influence and prayers of St. Francis.

"Behold I send you as sheep in the midst of wolves. Be ye therefore wise as serpents and simple as doves." (*Matthew* 10:16).

"He fought in the Crusade, in which he and he alone emerged the victor."[1]

The Fifth Crusade: "All in all, it was a dreary episode, relieved only by the presence of Francis of Assisi, whom Pelagius reluctantly permitted to cross the lines, where he was courteously received by al-Malik al-Kamil."[2]

1. Arnaldo Fortini, *Nova Vita di San Francesco* (Roma: Carucci Editore, 1981) p. 14.
2. "Crusades" (2007), in *Encyclopædia Britannica*. Retrieved April 19, 2007, from Encyclopædia Britannica Online: http://www.britannica.com/eb/article-235538

Table of Contents

Acknowledgments

Before mentioning those people to whom I am grateful, it is important to make a preliminary observation, in view of the potentially controversial nature of the topic of this book. My acknowledgement of someone's kind assistance and contribution to the research or writing of this book in no way is meant to signify that this person agrees with my viewpoints or conclusion. In other words, any name appearing in the acknowledgements should not be construed as an endorsement of my opinions.

First I would like express my heartfelt appreciation to Fr. Angelus Shaughnessy, O.F.M. Capuchin, who graciously consented to write the Preface for this book.

Special kudos go to Dick and Jan McCarthy, the Minister and Secretary respectively, of my Secular Franciscan family, the St. Clare Fraternity of Bethany Beach, Delaware. Dick and Jan read and commented on each chapter, and their valuable knowledge of St. Francis served them well as critics and inspirations.

A thank you to Brother Alexis Bugnolo, Editor of the Franciscan Archive on the web, for allowing me to use his translations from the Latin of St. Clare's "Testament" and St. Francis' "Canticle of Brother Sun," and also for his invaluable assistance and advice. Another thank you goes to Professor Emeritus James M. Powell, Syracuse University, for providing a copy of his Italian-language paper and also an unpublished manuscript on St. Francis and the Fifth Crusade. I am also grateful to Jeanette Salerno, novelist and writer, and to her sister Joan, for their invaluable suggestions over the past two years as they shared this journey.

I have used the 1900-page *Omnibus* as the source for over twenty of the earliest Franciscan books and writings, which are cited in the footnotes as included in the *Omnibus*. Its full title is *St. Francis of Assisi: Writings and Early Biographies, English Omnibus of Sources for the Life of St. Francis,* Marion A. Habig, Editor. When a work is taken from the *Omnibus,* its original chapter and paragraph number are given, if available, so that the citations can be found elsewhere than in the *Omnibus*.

The Church at the time of St. Francis used the Latin Vulgate Bible, and the Vulgate has been used in this book (The Vulgate contains books from the Greek Septuagint, absent in non-Catholic bibles.) The translation of the Vulgate used here is the Douay-Rheims version. It is available online at: http://www.drbo.org/ and also in print from TAN Books and Publishers, Inc., Rockford, IL 61105, http://www.tanbooks.com.

Finally, when an Internet website is given as a reference, the name of the site is included along with its Internet address. Since web pages sometimes are removed, a search on the name of the site will hopefully turn up a similar reference.

Preface

If anybody in human history ever had the right approach to invite the Muslims to Jesus Christ, it was St. Francis of Assisi. He was a fearless man of God, on fire to share the truth and love of the God-Man to all the world, even to the most difficult assignment that could ever be given to any Christian. St. Francis was wise and prudent, willing to put his life on the line to bring everyone home to the embrace of our Heavenly Father. This most dangerous commission is given only to those who are qualified to be sent, after submitting their inspiration to the Lord in prayer and to their superiors in the Church for approval. Their goal is salvation for themselves and for all those invited to submit to the King of Kings and Lord of Lords.

The author of this volume is qualified to present his thesis for our reflection because his research has been thorough and he has known St. Francis now for many years, as he is a follower and student of the Franciscan way of life in the Secular Franciscan Order. His research is trustworthy and acceptable, without any undue bias in interpreting his original sources.

The subject is timely because the Muslim world in some places has taken a hard line against Christians, in some instances refusing to give them permission to worship in their customary way through the Holy Sacrifice of the Mass. Punishment, incarceration and death are the threats in some Muslim countries for those who would break their laws. When Mother Angelica in 1982 visited Pope John Paul II in Rome and presented him with a baby satellite dish, his only comment to her was: "Beware of the Muslims!"

And there was a certain foreboding to his voice. The example of St. Francis in confronting the Sultan of Egypt offers the *Eternal Word Television Network* and the world probably the best way possible to present Christianity to Muslims. St. Francis did not attack Mohammed! He presented Jesus Christ as the Son of the Living God without apology, even though the Moslems did not believe in the Holy Trinity. He did not ridicule any of the tenets of Islam. He established his credibility by truly *loving* those he was addressing. There is no other accepted entrée than this. St. Francis did all of the above, inspired by the Holy Spirit, to the point of working miracles. A Saint can do all that with the help of God. The Sultan recognized that St. Francis was a Saint who loved God very much; and even before that, was also convinced that St. Francis himself was loved by God. St. Francis was full of love for God and for all God's people, even those who at the present moment do not accept Him as their Saviour.

St. Francis wanted everyone to love the God revealed by Jesus Christ. He would go to the ends of the earth, make the most difficult sacrifices, endanger his own life, if only he "would bring one more soul to Heaven." Jesus came into this world to die and to rise, to give His life as a ransom for many. St. Francis would do the same, and he would invite his followers to do likewise. Some Franciscans went "among the Saracens and other infidels" explicitly for that purpose: to be martyrs for Christ in order to establish their witness before an unbelieving world. This is especially difficult when the ones you are praying for and working for call *you* "infidels" for not accepting *their* idea of God, and they have declared "holy war" on all infidels!

The most modern approach to conversion is to dialogue, dialogue, dialogue! I suppose this is the "human" approach to those who think so differently from us—accentuate the positive truths we have in common: protection for human life and love for Mary, whom we know is the Virgin Mother of God. Certainly crusades and wars will not bring the Muslims to conversion at this time. The passive approach—simply to be among the Muslims, if permitted, relying on our good example—may take a few more centuries to bring them to conversion. But if only we could be the saints our God has called all of us to be, perhaps we would have the credibility and the authenticity that emboldened St. Francis to do what he did. I guess that would be the miraculous approach nowadays; but as Mother Angelica would so often repeat: "If you want to do the miraculous, you had better be prepared to do the ridiculous." Become saints! Even at the risk of being a martyr!

I am delighted that the author could highlight the year 1219 in the life of St. Francis of Assisi to give extensive treatment to this study of the Christian-Muslim relationship. This is a rare and daring approach to the life of St. Francis and one that is so necessary in our world at this time. We still have much to learn from this humble little Poor Man from Assisi.

—Fr. Angelus Shaughnessy, O.F.M. Cap.
St. Clare of Assisi Fraternity, Clairton, PA
(Formerly with EWTN)
May 24, 2007
Our Lady Help of Christians

Introduction

"Notwithstanding the long time that has elapsed since the death of the Seraphic Father, the admiration for him, not only of Catholics, but even of non-Catholics, continues amazingly to increase for the reason that his greatness appears to the minds of men with no less splendor today than it did long ago."—Pope Pius XI.[1]

While this book includes a concise biography that unfolds St. Francis' own conversion story, it primarily focuses on his courageous attempt to preach the Gospel in the Middle East to the followers of Islam. It is his bold approach to evangelization at the risk of martyrdom the makes the story of St. Francis appeal to all believers. When this great man of God walked fearlessly straight into the Muslim encampment during a lull in the fighting of the Fifth Crusade, he had only one purpose. His intention was to save the souls of the Muslim Sultan and as many of his followers as possible by converting them to the Christian Religion.

He made such an impact with his preaching that the Sultan rebuffed some of his own religious advisors, the *imams,* who were insisting that Islamic law required that St. Francis and his companion must be beheaded. With God's grace, St. Francis was able to exert a profound influence on the Sultan and others because of the simplicity and confidence of his preaching. For St. Francis, Christianity was the Person of Jesus Christ, and conversion to the Christian Religion was fundamentally conversion to belief in Jesus Christ as the Son of God.

St. Francis of Assisi and the Conversion of the Muslims is divided into three parts for the convenience of the reader. The mission of St. Francis to the Muslims is the subject of the central section of the book, i.e., Part II. This section may be read as a stand-alone piece for those interested only in this aspect of his life. Wrapped around this special focus on his encounter with Islam are Parts I and III, which comprise a concise biography of the Saint. Part I focuses on his early life, his conversion, and the founding of the three Franciscan Orders, whereas the closing Section deals primarily with the gift of the stigmata and his final days. These two Sections provide an overview of his spiritual journey, highlighting representative aspects and key events of his life.

I have primarily consulted early thirteenth-century writings (in translation) to arrive at an account of these major events that is reasonable and as accurate as possible. Bits and pieces of the story of St. Francis' journey to the Middle East and his visit with the Sultan are strewn throughout this early source material. I have attempted to include all of these scattered items in Part II, in order to build a cohesive and chronological account of this period of his life. One of the exceptions to the use of ancient sources is my reliance on the important Italian-language biography of the Saint produced in the middle of the last century by the former mayor of Assisi, Arnaldo Fortini.[2]

When studying the thirteenth-century writings on St. Francis, it soon becomes apparent that there are variations and interpretations of specific incidents in his life. This occurs quite often, despite the fact that those who personally knew either the Saint or his companions composed these works shortly after his death. Sources may disagree on a variety of issues, such as the year of St. Francis' birth, the content of his dreams, the nature of his visions, or the exact names of his followers. In some cases, I have been forced to present what I considered to be the most representative or reliable description of events, while trying to be as accurate as possible. My intention throughout has been to provide a concise, readable biography, with the primary emphasis and focus on St. Francis' mission to the Muslims, the major thrust of the book.

Unlike certain fashionable attempts to demythologize Catholic Saints and figures, I have not endeavored to remove the halo from St. Francis! To reduce this Saint to a glorified social worker, a nature lover, or "the first hippie" is a great disservice to his true heritage. St. Francis is generally recognized as the first person to have received the wounds of Christ, called the stigmata. He founded the three original Franciscan Orders—the Friars Minor, the Poor Clares, and the Secular Franciscans, known as the Third Order of St. Francis. His impact on the medieval world was immense, and he fulfilled the commission personally entrusted to him by Christ: "Rebuild My house." He was loyal to the papacy and to the Church hierarchy and was neither disobedient nor a rebel of any sort. He was a man of prayer and a great apostle, responsible for countless conversions and healings. When he traveled to Egypt with the Crusaders, his goal was to preach Christ to the Muslims at the risk of martyrdom. His level of spirituality was so elevated and so pleasing to God that all God's creatures paid him homage.

This work is not meant to be a study of the various interpretations which biographers and historians have given on the way St. Francis wished his followers to interact with Islam. However, mention must be made of a contemporary revisionist movement which alleges that St. Francis' primary goal was not to preach the saving Gospel of Christ to the Muslims. In fact, before I began researching this book, I had no idea that some students of St. Francis were putting such an interpretation on his relations with Islam, suggesting that his real purpose was to encourage his friars to pursue a passive form of peaceful coexistence, while living in subjection to the Muslims.

The earliest sources indicate that St. Francis included the followers of Islam in the general category of "unbelievers" and "infidels" who were in need of conversion to the God of Christianity in order to be baptized and saved. Preaching Christ at the risk of martyrdom was not something to be shirked for a committed disciple like St. Francis. But the revisionist movement offers a contrasting interpretation, which de-emphasizes and obscures St. Francis' mission of saving souls by bringing them to Christ and the True Religion. The crux of this false hypothesis is that St. Francis had no overriding desire to proselytize the Muslims, preferring instead that his friars live in peace and subjection to them. One of the major proponents of this hypothesis is the Dutch teacher and scholar J. Hoeberichts, who admits in his book, *Francis and Islam,* that while teaching in Pakistan he was influenced by "Asian theologians of liberation."[3] (Liberation Theology, often reproved by the Vatican, appears more concerned with the economic plight of the poor than with their spiritual needs and salvation.)

Hoeberichts summarizes his position by stating that St. Francis' primary objective for his Order was that the friars should be "subject to the Saracens, staying among them without any feeling of superiority and sharing their work and food with them."[4] In another place he states, "In Francis' approach, preaching did not take priority."[5] Further, according to Hoeberichts, martyrdom was also not a consideration: "Francis clearly indicated that he and his brothers were not motivated by a desire for martyrdom," but should "avoid arguments and disputes and be subject to the Saracens for God's sake."[6]

Even the publisher of the English translation of Hoeberichts' book admits in its Foreword that the author's view is a "radical reinterpretation."[7] This reinterpretation flies in the face of the descriptions of St. Francis' preaching to the Muslims provided by the original sources and reported in Part II of the present book. But these accounts are no obstacle for Hoeberichts; instead, he makes the incredible assertion that "the stories about the disputes between Francis and the Saracens must be banished to the land of fables."[8]

St. Francis did, in fact, in his Rule of 1221, mention that one way his friars could conduct themselves among the Muslims was to simply confess themselves to be Christians and avoid arguments by living in peaceful subjection. However, this was not the primary objective of the Franciscan mission to Islam, but only applied to those brothers who had not yet discerned that it was God's will for them openly to preach Christianity. Thus, one way of conduct was essentially passive, without the risk of martyrdom that could come by openly proclaiming Christ. The preferred way, however, was the active one of fulfilling Christ's commission to preach the Gospel fearlessly, which the early sources clearly document is the way that St. Francis acted with the Sultan in Egypt.

Hoeberichts reverses the priority of these two ways of approaching the Muslims. His thesis is aptly refuted by Professor Benjamin Kedar in his acclaimed work, *Crusade and Mission.*[9] Kedar clearly illustrates that there is a "tension" between what he sees as the two overriding motives for the Franciscan outreach to the Muslims—the longing for martyrdom and the desire to win converts by preaching. "But the individual missionary leaving for the lands of Islam had to make up his mind whether his foremost aim was to persuade the infidels of Christianity's truth, or to attain self-fulfillment by suffering death at their hands."[10] Living among them in passive subjection was not a major aim of the early Franciscan missionary.

There is no doubt that for St. Francis, preaching the word of God came first and foremost, and martyrdom was the risk that had to be taken—as well as the reward that might be proffered. St. Bonaventure affirms the fact that St. Francis was primarily interested in the conversion and salvation of souls. He writes in his *Major Life* of the Saint that St. Francis "used to say that nothing should take precedence over the salvation of souls, because it was for souls that the only-begotten Son of God hung upon the Cross."[11] Thus it would not be correct to say that St. Francis' purpose in reaching the Middle East was to obtain the palm of martyrdom for its own sake. It is equally misleading to assert that his goal was peaceful coexistence and subjection to the followers of Islam, in order to, in the words of Hoeberichts, "accept the Muslims in their otherness."[12]

A main intention of this book is to present the encounter of St. Francis with the Sultan of Egypt and his *imams* just as the original sources portray it. These stories speak for themselves plainly and simply, and are hopefully presented without any personal interpretation. Some of the Saint's frank words to the Sultan may seem harsh to present-day Christians who have repeatedly been exposed to a Modernist ecumenical approach, consisting of "an exchange of ideas," rather than the traditional preaching with the goal of converting the listener. Others may find it hard today to accept that someone would be willing to face death in order to bring Christ to unbelievers.

How successful was St. Francis in his attempt to convert the Sultan to Christ? I offer my own answers to this crucial question at the conclusion of the book.

PART ONE
The Founder

"He is seen to go about careless and roughly clad, begging his food from door to door, not only enduring what is generally deemed most hard to bear, the senseless ridicule of the crowd, but even to welcome it with a wondrous readiness and pleasure. And this because he had embraced the folly of the cross of Jesus Christ, and because he deemed it the highest wisdom. Having penetrated and understood its awful mysteries, he plainly saw that nowhere else could his glory be better placed."
—Pope Leo XIII, *Auspicato Concessum,* no. 11.*

---

* http://www.vatican.va/holy_father/leo_xiii/encyclicals/documents/hf_l-xiii_enc_17091882_auspicato-concessum_en.html.

Chapter 1

Youthful Dreams of Knighthood

THE future Saint was born and baptized in 1182 as Giovanni di Bernardone, in Assisi, the city he made famous—an ancient mountain town nestled in the Umbria region of Central Italy. Umbria, one of the smallest of the twenty regions of Italy, is located in the geographical heart of the peninsula. Pietro (Peter), the baby's father, was a successful cloth merchant who was away on business, perhaps in France, at the time of his son's birth. Upon his return, he had the child's name changed from Giovanni to Francesco (Francis). Peter had met his wife Pica in Provence, and often made business trips to France, and it is thought that these were reasons he changed the boy's name to Francesco—"the Frenchman." At the time, the name was considered unique and unusual.

As an adolescent and then as a young man up until his early twenties, Francis lived a worldly existence, taking little thought of heavenly matters. He worked in his father's dry goods shop and eventually might have become a successful merchant himself, although he was by nature quite generous and more inclined to spend rather than to save. His affable, outgoing personality made him quite popular among his peers, and he was often a leader in their youthful pastimes. Even older people noticed that the young lad possessed a certain nobility of soul. His mother Pica would ask her neighbors what they thought he would become, and she would prophetically supply the answer herself: "Know that he will be a son of God by the grace of his merits."[1]

There is a tradition that as a boy Francis was influenced by the Troubadours, composers and performers of songs and lyric poems written in praise of the ideals of true love and chivalry. These "wandering minstrels" flourished in Provence and southern France as well as in Spain and parts of Italy, leaving a lasting impact on medieval poetry and social mores. The Troubadours might have sparked Francis' childhood dreams of some day becoming a gallant knight and embarking on a distant crusade. Befitting his name, Francis even began to learn to speak a little French.

His exceptional generosity and kindness, especially toward beggars, indicated that the spirit of God was gently nudging the youth even before the occurrence of his dramatic conversion experiences. It was said that he could not refuse anyone who asked him for alms in God's name. The origin of this commitment came about one day in his father's shop as he was engrossed in his duties. A pauper came inside and asked for alms for the love of God. Francis was so preoccupied with completing his tasks on time that he hurriedly shooed the hapless mendicant out of the store, sending him away empty-handed. Then God's grace touched his conscience, and he thought to himself that if this needy soul had sought charity in the name of some great worldly prince or king, he would have given him something. Instead, the man had asked in the name of the King of Kings, and he was too busy to help him! Thinking of these things with shame in his heart, he ran out the door after the beggar and bestowed on him a generous alms. After this, he resolved always to give what he could to anyone who asked him for charity in the name of God.[2, 3]

The Most High proceeded with His great work of preparing the soul and conscience of young Francis by visiting him with sickness and imprisonment. In 1202 hostilities broke out between Assisi and its traditional rival, the nearby city of Perugia. Francis was involved in a skirmish known as the Battle of Collestrada, in which Perugia was the victor, and he was taken prisoner along with many of his fellow townsmen. He remained in prison for a year before he was able to return home. Although he became acutely ill during his incarceration, his demeanor and spirits were lively, even to the point of causing annoyance to some of his fellow captives. One called him a fool for being so happy, and he replied that it was right that he should rejoice, because "The day will come when I shall be honored by the whole world."⁴

Ill health continued to afflict him even after his release, which was probably arranged after a ransom payment by his father to the Perugians. He suffered from a prolonged, low-grade fever, and during long periods of inactivity, his thoughts increasingly dwelled on the emptiness of worldly concerns and pastimes. Upon his recovery, he realized that he no longer admired many of the things in this life that he had previously coveted, although he was still not yet altogether detached from the world.

Even with this new disposition, his youthful dreams of knighthood still lingered. He soon had a brief encounter that expressed his magnanimous and chivalrous nature. One day he came across a knight from a prominent family who had fallen on hard times. The nobleman could not even afford garments worthy of his status in life and was so poorly dressed that he was "well nigh naked."⁵ The future Saint was moved by compassion not only for the man's poverty but also for his embarrassment. Francis at once took off some of his own costly attire and gave the clothes to the shabbily dressed knight. Here his nobility of soul was manifested, but little did he realize that giving up his garments out of compassion for his neighbor was but a preparation for his giving up everything for the love of God.

In the early part of the year 1205, a count of Assisi named Gentile was setting out for the south of Italy, to serve as a knight-in-arms for the cause of Pope Innocent III against certain German princes.[6] He intended to join the army of Walter of Brienne near Naples, who was having spectacular success in leading the Papal forces against the rebels. Francis saw this as his opportunity finally to realize his dreams of knighthood, and lost no time in procuring the necessary weapons, equipment and attire in order to join Count Gentile and Walter of Brienne.

But one evening, while on the road to join Brienne's forces, he had a vivid dream that greatly affected him. He dreamt that his father's house had been transformed into a splendid castle, decorated with shields, lances and saddles, and filled with knightly armor marked with the Sign of the Cross. He heard a voice which told him that all these arms were meant for him and his soldiers. As yet he had no inkling of the type of "soldiers" that this "voice" had in mind for him to lead. With the arrival of morning, he continued on his journey, his thoughts still filled with visions of worldly glory, until another dramatic dream occurred the very next night, at the town of Spoleto. This time the voice asked him which was the better choice, to serve the Lord or a servant, a rich man or a beggar? "Why are you choosing a beggar instead of God, who is infinitely rich?"[7] Francis now understood that these two dreams had been messages from God. He courageously put aside his thoughts of knighthood and military escapades and returned home to Assisi, his attention now inexorably drawn toward heavenly realities.

Upon his return, in a half-hearted manner he at first resumed partying with his companions from Assisi. Taking advantage of his natural generosity, they often made him the "master of revels," knowing full well that he would provide plentiful food and drink for his friends.[8] However, he was no longer attracted to such pastimes, and he only complied out of courtesy to them. Sometimes his mind appeared to wander off into a reverie while in their presence, and they teased him, thinking he had fallen in love and wished to marry. Without revealing the secret of his heart, he replied, "I shall bring home a bride, more beautiful, richer, and nobler than any you have ever seen."[9]

Eventually Francis withdrew completely from these worldly diversions and sought to spend more time alone in contemplation, trying to discover God's will for him. His desire to seek the Lord in a deeper way led him to frequent a hidden grotto near Assisi, where he passed long periods in intense prayer. He would only let one close friend accompany him, who would wait outside the cave until Francis emerged, sometimes visibly fatigued. These early efforts at prayer were a true straining forward to find God, as vividly described by the Apostle Paul: "But one thing I do: forgetting the things that are behind, and stretching forth myself to those that are before, I press towards the mark, to the prize of the supernal vocation of God in Christ Jesus." (*Philippians* 3:13-14).

At about this time Francis made a pilgrimage on his own to St. Peter's in Rome, where he venerated the first Pope and Prince of the Apostles at the altar dedicated to him. But Francis was so dismayed at the paltry offerings left in honor of St. Peter that he threw down a generous handful of coins before the altar. They clattered noisily about, attracting the attention of the visitors and pilgrims, who were astonished at such an expression of charity. Exiting the basilica, he came upon a group of beggars who frequented the vestibules, hoping for some alms from the pilgrims. Francis' love for poverty, which had been steadily growing in his heart, was already so fervent that he eagerly exchanged his fine clothing for the rags of one of the unfortunates. He spent the rest of the day as one of them, asking for alms and joyfully sharing their meager food, before embarking on the journey home. The Lord's grace continued to expand his heart and mind. One day in prayer, he discerned that God wished him to deny himself totally by conquering his self-will, and by considering as bitter and unpleasant whatever he had once loved. He sensed the Lord telling him that if he did this, ". . .the things that formerly made you shudder will bring you great sweetness and content."[10] Francis made a resolution to follow this counsel, and shortly after his decision to embark on this new way of conduct, his resolve was dramatically put to the test.

A serious problem in Italy and throughout Europe during the Middle Ages, especially during the time of the Crusades, was leprosy. The festering sores, decayed tissues and disfigurement of the victims caused them to be shunned and isolated, and they were often forced to wear signs and ring bells warning of their approach.[11] The general populace feared and avoided them, and Francis was no exception in the way he had treated lepers. As he was riding through the countryside around Assisi, he unexpectedly came upon one of these sad wretches he so loathed. He immediately experienced a wave of aversion and disgust at the sight of the disfigured man. But he remembered his resolution, and overcoming himself, he dismounted and approached the poor creature. The leper extended his hand to receive some coins, which Francis readily gave to him. Then the budding saint meekly lowered his head, and bending forward, bestowed a gentle kiss on that same diseased hand. As the leper thanked him, Francis quickly mounted his horse and was on his way once more. He turned to look around, and although he was riding in an open field with a clear view on all sides, there was no sign of the leper anywhere.

This incident radically changed his outlook toward these

poor unfortunates, and he soon was making visits to the leper hospitals and forbidden places where they were housed, giving alms to each one, kissing them on their hands and on their mouth. In this way he conquered his life-long aversion to them, and began to experience sweetness where he had once tasted only bitterness, as the Lord had foretold. Francis himself wrote in his *Testament*, "When I was in sin, the sight of lepers nauseated me beyond meas-ure; but then God himself led me into their company, and I had pity on them."[12]

God had already led the Poor Man of Assisi—*the Poverello*—far along on his journey toward detachment and poverty, but he was still clothed in the garments of the world. However, the day was fast approaching when Francis would make a final and definitive break with his past, his family and his earthly attachments. He would dramatically shed the trappings and embellishments of this life, in order to dedicate himself completely, body and soul, to living the Gospel of his crucified Saviour.

Chapter 2

"Francis, Go, Repair My House."

I T was now the Autumn of 1205. Francis spent much of his time wandering about the idyllic Umbrian foothills of Assisi, contemplating God and the beauty of His creation, while at the same time pondering his own uncertain future. Not far from the town, he came upon an old crumbling chapel dedicated to St. Peter Damian, commonly known as the church of San Damiano. Francis reverently entered, and found himself completely alone in the aging edifice, since the priest assigned to it was away at the time. This priest had often witnessed Francis in his more carefree days carousing about the city, and would have been quite surprised to see the young man step into the chapel and kneel devoutly before the crucifix. It was a large Byzantine painting, depicting Jesus suspended on the Cross while still alive, His expressive dark eyes exuding a peaceful and calm otherworldly resignation. The image of Jesus was surrounded by smaller, colorful figures and symbols related to the story of salvation. Francis was soon deep in prayer before this beautiful icon of Our Lord.[1]

As he contemplated the countenance of the crucified Christ, he saw the lips on the image begin to move and clearly heard the voice of Jesus addressing him by name: "Francis, go, repair My house, which, as you see, is falling completely to ruin."[2] This command was repeated twice more in succession, and Francis was understandably fearful and overwhelmed. He remained motionless, becoming rapt in

10

prayer—perhaps in ecstasy. When he returned to himself, he knew he must begin at once to accomplish what the Lord wanted. But first he sought out and found the priest who was in charge. He gave him some money, asking that an oil lamp remain lighted before the miraculous San Damiano crucifix.

Francis interpreted the message to "repair my house" in a literal sense, as a directive to fix the ruined chapel of San Damiano. He hastened back to Assisi, furtively obtained some reams of fine, colorful cloth from his father's dry-goods shop, and proceeded on horseback to the market town of Foligno. There he sold both horse and textiles, and went back on foot to bring the money he had obtained to the priest at San Damiano, so that repairs on the church could begin. But this wise prelate would not accept the gains from Francis' transactions in Foligno, because he knew well of the temper of the young man's father. Francis, having already learned something about detachment, was unwilling to keep the money himself, so he disdainfully threw it on a windowsill. This kindly priest, however, was agreeable to letting Francis live at his home near the church.

Peter Bernardone, Francis' father, began a search for him. It was not so much an effort to find his missing son, as to recover the money obtained from the Foligno transactions. Francis, who still lacked complete trust in God and in his own calling, went into hiding, concealing himself in a cave for about a month. At least one friend or relative knew where he was, since on occasion some food and water were secretly taken to him. Although subsisting in this manner weakened him physically, the confinement allowed him to devote long, uninterrupted hours to prayer and meditation. Gradually his faith began to strengthen, and enlightened by God's grace, he realized his cowardice. Fortified by a renewed confidence in Christ and brimming with spiritual joy, the now unkempt lad emerged from the cave and strode boldly into

Assisi—only to be met with ridicule and mockery by his friends and neighbors.

As the haggard, disheveled servant of God passed them along the streets, the townspeople greeted him with mud, dirt, and stones, treating him as if he had gone mad. Hearing the commotion, his father ran out and grabbed the young man, dragging him into the family home. When reasoning with his son did not work, he beat him and chained him in the cellar, much to the chagrin of Francis' mother, Pica. His father felt that it was better to keep this wayward son out of sight, rather than have him ruin the family's reputation by wandering the streets as a useless vagrant.

Some days later, the elder Bernardone was called away on business. Pica saw this as her opportunity to set the boy free, which she did, although it meant that she would have to face the wrath of her husband. Francis, exulting in his newfound liberty, joyfully made his way back to San Damiano.

When Peter returned and found Francis missing, he initially vented his anger on Pica, and then set out in an uproar to retrieve Francis in order to bring him before the local bishop. He had already tried to get the municipal authorities to make Francis turn over the Foligno proceeds, but they would not intervene, contending that his son was now a ward of the Church and not under civil jurisdiction.[3] This time Francis went out to meet his father, not cowering and hiding as he had done before, and respectfully accompanied him to the Bishop's residence.

There, in front of many witnesses said to be present, the pair appeared before Guido, the Bishop of Assisi. The Bishop calmly explained to Francis that it would be wrong to restore San Damiano using funds that had been obtained by selling items not belonging to him. He exhorted the young man to have complete trust in God, who would faithfully provide all that would be necessary to rebuild the church. Francis now realized it had been wrong to sell his father's possessions, even for a good cause. He willingly agreed that the money should be returned to him. Francis then proceeded to carry out one of the most dramatic gestures ever recorded in the long history of Christendom. He insisted that not only the money, but every item in his possession that had come from his family should be returned to his father, including the very clothes he was wearing. To the astonishment of all, he removed his fine garments one by one, including his trousers, and gave them to Peter Bernardone. He was left now with the only piece of clothing that was rightfully his, a hair shirt that he had been secretly wearing. He accompanied this shocking deed with these words to the speechless onlookers: "From now on I will say 'Our Father who art in Heaven,' and not father Peter Bernardone."[4, 5]

The Bishop understood immediately that only the Spirit of God could have inspired such a courageous act. Francis had definitively chosen to follow in the footsteps of the Master, who was himself stripped of everything, as He hung virtually naked on the cross. Bishop Guido's sympathies from then on were with the Poverello, the Poor Man of God. He drew the young man toward him and tenderly covered him within the folds of his own bishop's mantle, an act of charity symbolizing that Francis would now be embraced and protected by the Church. The Bishop asked some of his assistants to fetch something for Francis to wear, and they returned with an old worn-out tunic belonging to a farmhand. Francis joyfully accepted it, and with a piece of chalk drew a cross upon it.[6]

He had irrevocably committed himself to leaving the world and all its trappings behind and was now clothed with the sign of Christ Crucified before the eyes of God and man. There would be no turning back for Francis, and he was faithful to his calling for the rest of his life, mindful of the Gospel precept: "Jesus said to him: No man putting his hand to the plough, and looking back, is fit for the kingdom of God." (*Luke* 9:62).

Chapter 3

Herald of the Great King

NOW that he was truly detached from the world, Francis spent the first days of this glorious freedom singing the praises of God, while strolling about the charming hills and valleys that grace the countryside of Assisi. He was so full of joy and confidence that, when some robbers accosted and questioned him, he merrily replied, "I am the Herald of the Great King!"[1] They promptly pummeled him and threw him into a snow-filled ditch. Francis blithely climbed out, still praising God, and thought no more about his assailants after forgiving them from his heart.

He soon ventured upon the Benedictine monastery of San Verecondo, where he remained for a few days working as a kitchen helper and menial. Here the shabbily dressed stranger was despised, harassed and treated with scorn. Since these monks would not leave him in peace, he went forth from that place, seeking the silence of prayer and meditation elsewhere. He arrived at the town of Gubbio, where he met a previous acquaintance who was moved to compassion upon seeing Francis dressed in tatters. This kindly gentleman gave him one of his coats, along with a leather cincture, shoes, and a staff. While in Gubbio, Francis spent some time at a nearby leper colony, where he tended to the sores and lesions of these sad creatures, washing out the infected puss and tenderly kissing their wounds.

During this time the angel of the Lord had been tugging at his conscience, and his thoughts turned to the vision he

had experienced at San Damiano and to his duty to respond
to Christ's sacred commission to repair His church. It was
now summer of the year 1206; about nine months had
elapsed since that miraculous event.[2] He made his way back
to San Damiano and assured the resident priest that he now
had the blessing of the Bishop to proceed honestly with the
work. Building blocks were needed for the reconstruction
effort, and Francis went through Assisi asking for stones,
and then hauling the heavy slabs back to the chapel.

The priest sought to compensate him by preparing meals
that were somewhat in line with the fine foods that Francis
had been accustomed to while he was living at home. Francis, however, quickly recognized that this was not in keeping
with his desire for poverty and detachment, and he put an
end to such special treatment. Instead, despising the shame,
he went into town carrying a bowl and begging for scraps of
food. When he returned to San Damiano and sat down to eat
from the dish, he was filled with disgust at the unappetizing
mixture. Struggling to overcome himself, he conquered his
natural aversion and forced himself to eat; and the Lord,
pleased with His loyal servant, caused this bitter pottage to
taste like a savory meal.

Little by little, popular opinion of Francis among many of
the people of Assisi and the neighboring area began to
change from one of mockery and pity to one of admiration.
His spiritual joy was contagious, and some even began to
help him with the building project. He prophesied to them
that the church would some day be part of a convent of holy
virgins who would give great glory to the Lord. Within six
years this prediction was fulfilled to the letter, when St.
Clare of Assisi and her first followers made San Damiano
the home of their Order.[3, 4] The authenticity of this prophecy
is verified in the *Testament* of St. Clare, written in Latin a
few years before her death in 1253:

The Saint himself, as one not yet having friars nor companions, immediately after his own conversion, when he was building the Church of San Damiano ... prophesied on account of great gladness and illumination of the Holy Spirit concerning us (Poor Clares), which the Lord afterwards fulfilled.

For ascending at that time upon a wall of the said church, to certain poor folk dwelling there nearby, he spoke in the French tongue, shouting: "Come and help me on the work of the Monastery of San Damiano, since there will one day be ladies there, whose famous life and holy comportment will glorify Our Heavenly Father throughout His entire Holy Church."[5]

After San Damiano had been restored, Francis moved on to another isolated, ruined church. This house of worship, built in honor of St. Peter, was called San Pietro della Spina; it, too, was repaired by Francis. Next, he came upon a poor, deserted chapel of truly ancient origin that was dedicated to Our Lady, called the Portiuncula, or Little Portion. He was immediately attracted to it, since he was already greatly devoted to the Mother of God.

This tiny church, belonging to the Benedictines of Mt. Subasio, lay in ruins and was totally abandoned, except for herdsmen, who used it as a shelter in bad weather. According to tradition, it had been constructed in the fourth century by a group of hermits from Palestine, who placed within it relics from the sepulcher of the Blessed Virgin.[6] The Portiuncula was also known as Our Lady of the Angels because it was said that the singing of angels was frequently heard there. When Francis began the work of restoring this church, which is located on a plain only about a mile from Assisi, he

was so enamored of its holiness that he decided to live
nearby in an abandoned hut. The Portiuncula was the third
chapel that he had undertaken to restore.

Francis' biographer, St. Bonaventure, considered that
these churches symbolized the three Orders that Francis
would found as he fulfilled Christ's command to repair His
Church—the Order of Friars Minor for priests and brothers,
the Poor Clares for women, and the Third Order of St. Francis, instituted primarily for the laity.[7] The Order of Friars
Minor is joined today by two offshoots, the Capuchins and
Conventuals. These branches of the First Order emerged over
time as a witness to the vibrant power of the Franciscan
charism. In addition, the Third Order Regular now exists for
Third Order members who wish to live in community.

On February 24, 1208, Francis asked the priest from San
Damiano to come and offer Mass at the Portiuncula for the
feast of the Apostle St. Matthias. The Gospel reading was
from the tenth chapter of St. Matthew, describing the words
of Jesus as he commissioned the Twelve Apostles to begin
their apostolic mission.[8]

> And going, preach, saying: The kingdom of heaven is
> at hand. Heal the sick, raise the dead, cleanse the lep-
> ers, cast out devils: freely have you received, freely
> give. Do not possess gold, nor silver, nor money in
> your purses: Nor scrip for your journey, nor two coats,
> nor shoes, nor a staff; for the workman is worthy of
> his meat. And into whatsoever city or town you shall
> enter, inquire who in it is worthy, and there abide till
> you go thence. And when you come into the house,
> salute it, saying: Peace be to this house. And if that
> house be worthy, your peace shall come upon it; but if
> it be not worthy, your peace shall return to you. And
> whosoever shall not receive you, nor hear your words:

going forth out of that house or city shake off the dust from your feet. (*Matthew* 10:7-14).

This passage of the Holy Gospel made a profound impact on Francis. It seemed that these words, spoken so long ago, were directly addressed to him, instructing him to live in poverty while preaching the kingdom of God. After asking the priest to explain the reading to him to be sure he understood it, Francis immediately and joyfully responded to the message. He cried out: "This is what I wish, this is what I seek, this is what I long to do with all my heart!"[9] It was a transforming, pivotal moment in his life, as if Jesus had personally commissioned him, through this Scripture passage, to be one of His Apostles. God had been preparing Francis for this decisive stage in his journey, step by step over the past few years, creating a longing in his heart—a spiritual yearning that Francis had been unable completely to discern—until these words from Scripture were preached to him.

His first act was literally to clothe himself according to Christ's instructions, and he put away his staff, shoes and wallet. He donned the rustic, woolen tunic common to peasants, which was in the shape of a cross, and replaced his leather cincture with a cord of rope. Then, using plain and simple speech, he went out and began to preach the message of penance and the Gospel of peace to everyone whom he met. He started his orations with the greeting, "The Lord give you peace!"—a salutation that Francis later declared had been taught to him directly by the Lord. His words had the power of the Holy Spirit behind them, since he was a man who had personally experienced the God he was proclaiming. He immediately began to influence and inspire many of his hearers. Often those who were moved by his preaching had already witnessed his way of life, and they understood that Francis was truly living and practicing what he taught.

It was not long after the start of this public ministry that God began calling people to follow in the footsteps of Francis. The first of these was a wealthy nobleman and lawyer, Bernard of Quintavalle. Bernard had been deeply moved by the words and holiness of this angelic soul. Nevertheless, in order to resolve some doubts, one day he invited the itinerant preacher to his home for dinner and an overnight stay. He arranged to have an extra bed placed in his own bedroom, where an oil lamp remained lit during the night. Pretending to be asleep, he watched as Francis rose from his bed and knelt on the floor in fervent prayer. He could hear the words "My God and my all!" being repeated throughout the night, as Francis lifted his heart to the Lord incessantly. The next day Bernard, now convinced that he was in the presence of a man of true holiness, asked Francis if he could join him as a spiritual companion. The Poverello of Assisi was overjoyed, since he was given the grace to understand that the Lord was calling Bernard of Quintavalle to be the first of his followers.

Bernard told Francis that he intended to give away all his wealth; however, the two men wanted to be sure that this was God's will. They entered the church of St. Nicholas, located in the town of Assisi, and spent a long time there in prayer. Then Francis opened the book of the Gospels three times in honor of the Trinity to see if the Lord would reveal whether Bernard should give up all things.[*] The first opening revealed the words: "If thou wilt be perfect, go sell what thou hast, and give to the poor." (*Matthew* 19:21). On the second opening: "Take nothing for your journey." (*Luke* 9:3). The third time: "If any man will come after me, let him deny himself." (*Luke* 9:23). From this it was clear what the Lord wished

---

[*] Some sources report that Peter of Catania, another early follower of Francis, was also present, and that the parish priest of St. Nicholas opened and read the Missal for the three readings.

of Bernard, and he hastened to put into practice these counsels, by selling all he had, giving his money to the poor, and following Christ under the guidance of Francis. [10, 11]

Chapter 4

"The Lesser Brothers"

NEW brothers were added quickly once it became known that Francis had begun to attract followers. Among the first to join him were Brother Giles, who would eventually become known for his gift of sublime contemplation, and a priest, Father Silvester. Before long there were about a dozen of them, and they stayed in huts adjacent to Our Lady of the Angels church, the Portiuncula—cradle of the fledgling Order. They embraced Holy Poverty, refused to own property, and despised money. When they were unable to work for their food, they begged for their needs. Francis and his followers adopted this way of life because it imitated the Gospel poverty of Jesus and allowed them continually to lift their hearts up to God in unceasing prayer, both in common and privately. He taught his followers: "Know, my sons, that poverty is the special way to salvation; its fruit is manifold, but it is really well known only to a few."[1]

Francis began to call his brethren the lesser brothers, or Friars Minor. In choosing this name he was inspired by what is written in the book of Luke: "Fear not, little flock, for it hath pleased your Father to give you a kingdom." (*Luke* 12:32). Francis also had in mind the parable of the sheep and the goats, in which the Lord will come in glory to separate those who were good to Him while He was hungry, in need and in prison, from those who did nothing. When the doers of good deeds ask when they had ever seen Him hungry, thirsty and in want, they hear the answer: "Amen I say to you, as long as you did it to one of these my least brethren, you did it to me." (*Matthew* 25:40). For these reasons Francis wished his followers to be known as the least of the brethren.

Francis made use of the following explanation to encourage those brothers who were too ashamed to beg. He said that whenever, as the least of all, they asked a person for alms, they were actually performing an act of charity, because that person now had an opportunity to do a good work. He explained that those fortunate souls who gave alms to the friars earned merit toward their heavenly reward, by practicing "what will cause them to be glorified by the Supreme Judge."[2]

Francis drew up a short, elementary "Rule" of life for the friars, based on their simple way of living the Gospel—without possessions, in chastity and under obedience. To insure that they were in fact submissive to the desires of Holy Mother Church and to seek formal approval of their Rule, the tiny band of companions journeyed to Rome to seek an audience with the Pope. It was the spring of 1209 when the "lesser brothers" went forth to meet the greatest of the medieval Popes, Innocent III. This Pope was not only the spiritual leader of the Catholic Church, he was also the temporal ruler of large areas of central Italy, known as the Papal States, and would soon preside over the Fourth Lateran Council.

Providentially, Bishop Guido of Assisi happened to be in Rome at that very time. When he saw Francis arrive with all of his followers, he began to worry that they had decided to move away from Assisi, where they had already effected a marvelous change in the way of life of its citizens. Francis hastened to put Bishop Guido's mind at ease on this issue. But when he explained to the Bishop that the friars were in Rome in order to seek formal approval for their Gospel way of life, Bishop Guido expressed his concerns that this manner of living, without possessions or money, would be much too rigorous. Francis replied that if the brothers were to accept money and worldly possessions, these could become a source of disputes and contentions, hindering them from the love of God and neighbor. Possibly concerned about brigands and thieves who frequented the countryside, he added that owning possessions would mean that "we should also be forced to have arms to protect them."[3]

Bishop Guido decided to introduce Francis to an influential Cardinal, John of St. Paul, who became very impressed by the sincerity and piety of the poor man of Assisi and his band of brothers. He promised to arrange an audience for Francis and his friars with Pope Innocent III. One early account holds that Francis had already tried to meet with the Pope on his own and had been sent away.[4] However, at the meeting arranged by the Cardinal, the Holy Father attentively listened as Francis explained his way of life, and he was favorably impressed by the demeanor and holiness of the Poverello and his companions.

As had happened with Bishop Guido, the Pope also had strong reservations about granting approval to the Rule Francis was proposing, objecting that it was too rigorous and extreme. Many of the Cardinals he consulted felt the same way. Further, at that time, the major heresies of Albigensianism and Catharism were in full bloom in Catholic lands. Among other false doctrines, these movements proposed a dualism between good and evil, which had supposedly created spirit and matter, respectively, and they regarded matter and the physical world as intrinsically evil.[5] The Pope had even begun an armed Crusade against the Albigensians in France the year before. Consequently, some of the Curial Cardinals were concerned that Francis and his followers wished to embrace poverty for heretical reasons, considering material possessions as evil in themselves.[6]

Francis, however, was motivated by a desire to conform to

the way of Gospel poverty because it had been revealed to him as a means to draw closer to God. His embrace of "Lady Poverty" was a positive impetus stemming from his desire to follow in the footsteps of Jesus Christ, rather than being based upon a negative hatred of material things. In fact, his praise of God's creation and of His creatures, which would soon be manifested in his writings and life, was the antithesis of those heresies.

Cardinal John of St. Paul, seeing the hesitation of the Pope, addressed the Holy Father and the Curia with a warning that if they rejected the petition of Francis, they in effect would be rejecting the teaching of Christ. "Anyone who says that a vow to live according to the perfection of the Gospel contains something new or unreasonable or too difficult to be observed, is guilty of blasphemy against Christ, the Author of the Gospel."[7] The Holy Father, who only wished to be certain of the will of God in this matter, called an end to the deliberations, with a plea that prayers be offered to determine the Divine good pleasure.

The early Franciscan chronicles tell of a number of dreams and visions experienced by both Francis and the Holy Father during this time. The most important of these was the dream of Innocent III shortly after his meeting with Francis. In this dream, he found himself alone inside the Basilica and Palace of St. John Lateran, which at that time was the official Papal residence. He was looking upon all of its glorious architecture and artworks, when suddenly there was a great rumble, and the walls, columns and ceiling of the magnificent basilica began to collapse and topple. He closed his eyes in fright, but when he reopened them, he was astonished to see that the Lateran was still standing, thanks to a gigantic person who was supporting it with his shoulders. Awakening with a start, he realized that the giant holding up the Basilica in his dream was the little barefoot friar of humble demeanor, Francis of Assisi.

Now freed from his doubts, he willingly gave verbal approval to the first Rule of the Order, and permitted Francis and his followers to preach in public a simple message of repentance, while proclaiming the Good News of salvation. In effect, this was the very mission that Our Lord Himself had undertaken when he " . . . came into Galilee, preaching the Gospel of the kingdom of God, and saying: The time is accomplished, and the kingdom of God is at hand: repent, and believe the Gospel." (Mark 1:14-15).

Pope Innocent took the further step of admitting all of the brothers to the clerical state by conferring upon them the sacred rite of tonsure (shearing of the hair). Shortly thereafter, the first Franciscans departed from Rome carrying their approved Rule, having obtained from the Holy Father all that they had prayed for. In this way, on April 16, 1209, the Order of Friars Minor was canonically established. Unfortunately for the sake of history, copies of this first Rule, as originally written by Francis and orally confirmed by the Pope, have not been preserved, although attempts have been made to reconstruct it.[8]

Chapter 5

Rivo Torto

THE joyful band of brothers began their homeward journey and stayed for a short time near a small town north of Rome called Orte, where they lived in a deserted church for about two weeks before moving on. Francis was reluctant to remain there any longer because the enchantment of the picturesque countryside and the temptation to consider their residence a "possession" might weaken the resolve and commitment of their fledgling Order. Proceeding in the direction of Assisi, they came upon a ruined hovel that could barely accommodate them. This worthless hut, located at Rivo Torto, was ideally suited to these men of God, committed as they were to a life of prayer, poverty and mortification. Here they took up their abode. The place was so small that Francis had to write the name of every brother along the beams so that each would know where he should pray and take his rest, without disturbing anyone else.

During their sojourn at Rivo Torto, Francis would visit the nearby neighborhoods and hamlets, preaching the simple but powerful Gospel of repentance and a return to the love of God. Although he was strongly attracted to a hermit's life of prayer and solitude, he was beginning to feel that his true calling was to go out among the people in order to win souls for Christ. His bold and confident preaching attracted individuals of every age and rank—both men and women, laity and clerics. Even the learned were struck by the penetrating simplicity of his words. He spoke compassionately about love of God and neighbor and how to live peaceably with each other for God's sake. He talked plainly and "briefly about vice and virtue, punishment and glory, because on earth Our Lord Himself kept His words short," as he would later write in the Rule of 1223.[1]

Within the tiny shelter at Rivo Torto the brothers spent much of their time immersed in continuous prayer. Since they owned no liturgical books or writings, they meditated on Christ and His sufferings and praised God in His works and His creatures. As simple sheep before their spiritual father, they once asked St. Francis how they should pray. He exhorted them to persevere in the *Pater Noster*, the "Our Father," and to add words such as: "We adore Thee, O Christ, in all Thy churches in the whole world, and we thank Thee, because by Thy Holy Cross Thou hast redeemed the world."[2] He taught them to pay special honor to all priests, not considering any of their sins, "because I can see the Son of God in them and they are better than I."[3] But above all else, he wished the Blessed Sacrament to be worshipped and honored, "because in this world I cannot see the most high Son of God with my own eyes, except for His most holy Body and Blood."[4]

One Saturday evening Francis went up to Assisi alone, since he was to preach the next morning in the Cathedral. In preparation for his discourse, he spent the night absorbed in prayer. Around midnight at Rivo Torto, while some of the brothers were praying and the rest were sleeping, a mysterious object in the likeness of a fiery chariot entered through the door of the hut. It circled the room three times before it disappeared, terrifying and astonishing everyone. The chariot was surmounted by a brilliant globe of light, which illuminated the dark hovel like the sun, and also enlightened in a marvelous way the minds of all those present. In its mystical light, their consciences were laid bare, and they could read each other's hearts. At the same time it was revealed to them that the shining globe was the soul of Francis himself, who had become present in spirit to his companions by means of this vision. The miracle was permitted by God to strengthen the new Order, and to confirm and inspire the friars in their choice to follow Francis: "The friars realized that the Spirit of God dwelt in His servant Francis so abundantly that they need have no hesitation in following his life and teaching."[5, 6]

After they had been at Rivo Torto for some months, one day a boorish peasant and his donkey chanced upon the hut. Forthwith he and Brother Ass forced their way in and took up residence. Francis needed no further sign to persuade him to seek another place of refuge for himself and his companions—preferably a small church with a shelter nearby that could accommodate others wishing to join the Order. After unsuccessful attempts at obtaining permission from the Bishop of Assisi and from the canons of the Cathedral for the use of some humble chapel, he approached the monks at the Benedictine monastery of Mt. Subasio, overlooking Assisi.

There the abbot sympathized with their plight and permitted the brotherhood the use of the small chapel of the Portiuncula that Francis had repaired. Francis was overjoyed, since he loved this simple and poor church above all others, especially since it was dedicated to the Blessed Virgin as Our Lady of the Angels. In fact, it was revealed to him that the Blessed Lady herself considered this her dearest church, and he maintained that, "Of all the churches in the world that the Blessed Virgin loves, she bears the greatest love for this one."[7]

Chapter 6

The First Flower

I T was probably early in 1210 that Francis and his companions moved into huts adjoining the chapel of the Portiuncula. At that time there were only a small number of friars, but the Order would grow rapidly as Francis' reputation for sanctity spread throughout the surrounding area. Along with unmarried men, very often married couples and single women were attracted to this humble way of Gospel penitence and simplicity, and the Saint would eventually accommodate both of these classes of people in the Franciscan family.

During Lent of 1212, Clare (Chiara Offreduccio), a wellborn young maiden of Assisi, listened raptly as Francis preached a course of sermons at the church of San Giorgio. This eighteen-year-old girl had a reputation for holiness and piety, and as her spiritual life had developed, so had her distaste for worldly pursuits and disinclination for marriage. Her biographer Thomas of Celano portrays her lyrically as "a youth in age, but mature in spirit; steadfast in purpose and most ardent in her desire for divine love; endowed with wisdom, and excelling in humility."[1] To St. Bonaventure, "she shone like a radiant star, fragrant as a flower blossoming white and pure in springtime."[2]

Inspired by the preaching of Francis, her heart opened to new vistas, and she longed to lead a life of Gospel poverty and prayer in imitation of the friars. Clare wished to meet the thirty-year old Poverello, who had already heard about her own reputation for sanctity. In fact, it was Francis who initiated the first of their furtive meetings and promised to protect and guide Clare in her spiritual quest.[3] After a number of these clandestine visits, at which someone else was always present, Clare made the decision that she, too, would follow Christ by renouncing the world. On the evening of Palm Sunday in March of that year, she secretly left her home and hurried to meet Francis at the Portiuncula, as they had planned beforehand.

Accompanied by a trusted friend, Clare arrived safely at the tiny chapel, where they were greeted by Francis and his brothers carrying lighted candles. At a ceremony before the altar of Our Lady of the Angels, she made her life-long commitment to follow Jesus Christ under the guidance of Francis. During the rite, Francis sheared the long blond tresses (still preserved today) of the kneeling virgin. He then proceeded to vest her with a veil, and then with the rough tunic characteristic of the early Franciscans, to symbolize her embracing of poverty. Just as Francis had become a follower of the evangelical life of Jesus, Clare would soon emulate the hidden life of Our Lady.

The humble Portiuncula chapel was now like a little Bethlehem, cradle of the first two Franciscan Orders: the Order of Friars Minor for men, and the Poor Clares for the holy virgins. "Thus it is plain to see that the merciful Mother gave birth to both religious Orders in her own house."[4] But having Clare reside at the Portiuncula, home of the friars, was out of the question. Francis arranged to have her sheltered at the convent of the Benedictine nuns of St. Paul, in Basta Umbria, only a few miles from Assisi. Accompanied for safety by some of the brothers, she was greeted warmly upon her arrival at the convent by the resident nuns.

In the meantime, her family became furious when they realized what had occurred—they could not understand how someone of noble birth could abandon a promising future in order to follow a gaggle of vagabonds. In addition, what she was doing was without precedent, since no other woman had yet chosen Francis' way of life.

It was not long before Clare's relations, joined by some of her friends, boldly entered the convent chapel at Basta Umbria and tried to drag the determined heiress home by brute force. But Clare, clutching the altar linens and exposing her shorn head, proclaimed her intention never to be separated from her commitment to serve Christ. After she retreated into the nuns' living quarters, which were protected by Church edict from any outsiders, the meddlers tried to use reason and persuasive promises to induce her to change her mind. They carried on the struggle for many days, until her determination finally convinced the family that their entreaties were useless, and they departed.[5]

In order to provide Clare with greater solitude, Francis sent her to the Benedictine monastery of St. Angelo of Panzo, which lay close to Assisi on the slopes of Mt. Subasio. Not long after her arrival at this refuge, her fourteen-year-old sister Caterina, who would take the name in religion of Agnes, joined her. This led to a repeat of the struggles that had been fought over Clare—on the day after the arrival of Agnes, a dozen men physically dragged her from the convent. Agnes cried out to her sister for help, and Clare, prostrating herself in prayer, tearfully begged the Lord to protect her sister from these marauding relatives.

The men dragged her down the side of Subasio, ripping her clothes and pulling her hair out. She fell to the ground before a certain stream, and when the kidnappers tried to lift her to carry her over the water, their efforts were confounded by a wondrous miracle. Agnes' body suddenly became exceedingly heavy, and the entire group of men, exerting all their strength, could not budge her. Even some field workers and onlookers joined the assailants in the attempt to lift Agnes, and still she remained immoveable. Finally Clare arrived on the scene and entreated the family to depart and leave the barely conscious girl to her care. Realizing it was useless to persist, the angry relatives sulked away. As soon as they had gone, Agnes easily raised herself up, and with great joy the two sisters returned to the convent praising and thanking God.[6]

Clare and her sister Agnes had been at St. Angelo of Panzo for only a short time when Francis decided upon a further transfer, choosing a small dwelling abutting the church of San Damiano as their permanent residence. San Damiano belonged to the Benedictines, and he had obtained their permission to let Clare and her followers live and worship there. In this way, the prophecy Francis had made when he first rebuilt San Damiano was fulfilled: that it would one day be the dwelling place of holy virgins who would give great honor and glory to God!

The Second Order grew rapidly after this, and even Clare's mother, along with some other relatives, would eventually leave the world to join them. Francis provided them with a short written Rule of life and appointed Clare as their Superior. Within a short time there were more than a dozen maidens, and the Order of Poor Clares began to spread to other towns in Italy and beyond. But the Saint herself was destined to remain at San Damiano for the rest of her days, devoting more than forty years to a hidden life of prayer, while the fame of her sanctity spread throughout the world.

St. Clare's contemporary, the Franciscan friar Thomas of Celano, wrote an important biography of the Saint along with those he wrote on St. Francis. His small book, *The Life of St. Clare Virgin*,[7] relates the glorious episode of the day Clare and her sisters were miraculously protected from a band of Saracen (Muslim) fighters, who had stormed the convent at

San Damiano. The year was around 1240, well after the death of her spiritual father Francis. The emperor Frederick II and his hired bands of mercenaries, which included Saracens and Tartars, were ravaging and looting the towns and villages of central Italy. As the raiders neared Assisi, the Saracen contingent headed for the church and convent of San Damiano. The danger was imminent and frightful, since these Saracens were "a mean people who thirst for Christian blood and attempt even the most brazen atrocities."[8] The general perception Christians had of Muslims during that era is apparent in this description of them by Celano.

Scaling the surrounding barricades, the Saracens shamelessly entered the confines of the cloister that housed Clare and her sisters in Christ. Clare was seriously ill and bedridden at the time. When the nuns rushed into her cell in desperation over the invaders, she commanded them to carry her directly to the front door along with "the ivory-encased silver box in which they devoutly kept the Body of the Holy of Holies."[9] Then, in full view of the enemy, she prostrated herself before Jesus in the Host, praying for deliverance for herself and her sisters.

Hoping against hope as the Muslims drew closer, she clearly heard the voice of her merciful Spouse declare: "I will always defend you." Mindful of the terrible danger to Assisi, Clare then begged for the safety of that city, which had always provided for the sisters. She then heard Christ reply that Assisi would be protected, in spite of some damage. Rejoicing, Clare told her companions to place all their trust in God, who would shield them from every harm. Almost immediately, the astonished Saracens, bewildered by the courage of this holy woman, withdrew from San Damiano in confusion. Perhaps they, too, had heard the mysterious voice, since Clare warned the sisters who had heard it to tell no one until after her death.

Chapter 7

Bearers of Peace

ALTHOUGH Francis and Clare met only infrequently once she had been cloistered within the San Damiano convent, she did play an important part in one of the major decisions affecting the course of his ministry. Francis had always been drawn toward the interior life and would have been quite content to dedicate most of his time to prayer and contemplation. On the other hand, he also had a wonderful gift for preaching. He could effectively communicate to others his love of God and inspired in many the desire to make the radical commitment to follow Christ in the way of Holy Poverty. He felt torn between these two callings and realized that he had to determine which way of life God wanted him to follow, the active or the contemplative.

In order to discern God's plan for him, and unwilling to rely on his own efforts, he called upon one of his companions, Brother Masseo.[1] This brother was sent to visit Clare at San Damiano. Following Francis' wishes, Masseo asked Clare to join in prayer with one of her sisters in religion, who was noted for the gift of holy simplicity. Together the two were to ask the Lord God to reveal whether Francis should be primarily engaged in preaching or in contemplation. As soon as Brother Masseo took his leave of Clare, he went up to Mount Subasio. There he located Fr. Silvester, the "Priest Brother," who often stayed alone on that mountain, spending long hours in meditation. Since Francis had great confidence in him, Fr. Silvester was also requested to

35

ask what the Lord's will was for the Poverello.

Fr. Silvester immediately began to pray about this and was quickly favored by God with an answer. Brother Masseo, who was still nearby, was asked to give Francis the message that his calling was not to the contemplative life; instead, he was to go out into the world and bring the good news of Christ to the people. Brother Masseo then went back to San Damiano, and there he found out that Clare and the other sister had received precisely the same revelation as Fr. Silvester.

Returning to the Portiuncula, Masseo sat down for a meal with Francis, after which the two brothers walked into the nearby woods. There, in the natural surroundings he loved so much, Francis solemnly and humbly knelt down and asked Masseo to relate to him what had been revealed concerning the Lord's will for him. The brother replied that both Clare and Fr. Silvester had received the same answer—that Francis should go about the world preaching, because God "did not call you for yourself alone but also for the salvation of others."[2]

As soon as God's will for him was revealed, Francis accepted it without hesitation. He wasted no time in responding to this call and joyfully went forth once again to preach penance in the neighboring towns and villages. This important juncture in his life probably took place in mid-1212, since it occurred after Clare's abandonment of the world earlier that year, and most likely before Francis set out to preach the Gospel to the Muslims in the Middle East—a journey that he undertook for the first time in the second half of 1212.

His zeal and the power of his speech in announcing the Good News was so great that many amazing—and now legendary—stories of his ability to communicate with birds and other animals began to appear. According to some of the earliest sources, once he was committed to preaching the Gospel message in earnest, the simplest creatures of God's creation were drawn toward him. Francis went forth as if Jesus had empowered him to take literally the command He had given to His first disciples: "And he said to them: Go ye into the whole world, and preach the Gospel to every creature." (*Mark* 16:15). It is said that Francis even addressed the flowers of the field, inviting them to "praise the Lord as though they were endowed with reason."[3]

To cite just one example, his biographers—Celano, St. Bonaventure, and the author of the *Little Flowers*—all recount a marvelous episode involving a flock of raucous swallows, although not agreeing on whether it was at Alviano or Cannara.[4, 5, 6] While none of these sources provides a date, the *Little Flowers* places this event as occurring immediately after Francis' commitment to the active life, which probably occurred in 1212. When Francis arrived at the village to preach, he gathered the populace around him and asked for silence. However, a large group of birds was nesting in the area, and their loud and cheerful chirping made it difficult for him to be heard. Turning in the direction of the frolicking swallows, Francis spoke directly to them, informing them that they had been talking long enough and it was now his turn to speak. He commanded the creatures to "Listen to God's word and be quiet until the sermon is over."[7] To the astonishment of the townspeople, the noisy, twittering, flock immediately calmed down, making nary a sound nor movement until Francis had finished his sermon.

The news of this miracle quickly spread throughout the area and beyond. The people of the town where this occurred were so moved at what they had witnessed that, then and there, they wanted to leave everything behind and follow in the steps of the Poor Man of Assisi. But he discouraged them from abandoning their homes and their village, promising that he would find a way to help them in their quest for salvation.

The *Little Flowers* relates that it was on this occasion at Cannara that the Poverello began to consider organizing a new Order, an Order for lay people, which would allow them to continue to live in their own homes and villages while pursuing the path of sanctity.[8] Fortini, Francis' major 20th-century biographer, also cites Cannara as the site of the events which inspired Francis to found this new Order.[9] (On the other hand, it should be pointed out that there are numerous other cities, and even particular individuals, that vie for the distinction of being the place where his Third Order was started.)

Over the door of a church in Cannara rests an ancient stone plaque on which is inscribed in Latin: "Sacred to Master Francis, who instituted the Order of Secular Penitents in this town before doing so anywhere else."[10] Originally called the Brothers and Sisters of Penance, this organization for people living in the world is commonly known today as the Secular Franciscan Order. Intended for the laity—men or women, single or married—its members continue to pursue their lives within society instead of renouncing their worldly goods and primary state of life. Secular clergy (those not belonging to a religious order) may also join, as have many Popes and bishops. Secular Franciscans, or Tertiaries (members of the "Third Order"), as they are also known, do not take formal vows, but do have a structured spiritual formation program they must follow prior to becoming professed Third Order members.

In 1221, the official Rule for the Third Order was approved by Pope Honorius III. In all likelihood, it was based on an informal Rule for Tertiaries previously drawn up by Francis, which had been in use for many years. Thus, although the year 1221 is the date of the canonical foundation of the Third Order, it had existed in seed form since 1212, the year Francis first began in earnest "to preach the

Gospel to every creature." It may even have originated as early as 1209, a date favored by some scholars.[11, 12] It is important to note that historically, Francis was not the first to institute an Order for lay people, but in his time the concept was still relatively new and uncommon.

An intriguing aspect of that early Rule of 1221, and of a later Rule from 1289, was the provision that Seculars should refrain from bearing arms. The 1221 Rule contained a very general statement to the effect that: "They are not to take up lethal weapons, or bear them about, against anybody."[13] The Rule of 1289 was modified to specify that weapons could be wielded in defense of God or country: "Let the brothers not carry offensive weapons with themselves, unless in defense of the Roman Church, the Christian Faith, or their country, or with the permission of their ministers."[14] In contrast, the current Rule of the Secular Franciscan Order makes no mention at all of arms or weapons, but instead characterizes Tertiaries as peacemakers: "Mindful that they are bearers of peace which must be built up unceasingly."[15]

In addition to the provision against bearing arms, another paragraph of the 1221 Rule enjoined Tertiaries to refrain from pledging formal oaths, with certain exceptions.[16] These prohibitions on oath-taking and bearing arms had immediate and lasting consequences on the society of the time. In a letter written by Pope Honorius III to the Bishop of Rimini, on December 16, 1221, mention is made of an attempt by the civil authorities of Rimini to force the local Third Order members to take an oath to defend the city by the force of arms if necessary. In the letter, the Pope asks the Bishop to stand up for the rights of the Order against the demands of the secular authorities.[17]

The Third Order's restrictions on weapons and oaths had the marked effect of diminishing the frequency of the clan and feudal wars and battles that were common in that era.[18]

Feudal lords and land barons soon discovered that they were unable to obtain sufficient men for their private armies, since potential recruits were unwilling to swear an oath of loyalty or take up weapons on their behalf. In fact the impact was so far-reaching that some historians claim that the establishment of the Third Order for lay people was a significant factor in the decline of the feudal system of the Middle Ages. "The beneficent influence of the secular Third Order of St. Francis cannot be highly enough appreciated. Through the prohibition against carrying arms, a deadly blow was given to the feudal system and to the ever-fighting factions of Italian municipalities."[19]

Thus the year 1212 was significant for a number of reasons in the life of the thirty-year old Francis. First, it witnessed the establishment of the Second Order, founded for women who wished to leave the world and follow his way of life—an Order also known as the Poor Clares. Shortly thereafter came his definitive commitment to a life of evangelical preaching. Although the exact date that Francis first conceived the Third Order has been lost to history, the success of his preaching underscored the need for such an intermediate Order, which could accommodate men and women who by choice or necessity would remain in the world. A further development resulting from Francis' zeal to spread the Gospel message was his determination to take his missionary activity into non-Christian lands. This desire, too, first bore fruit in 1212 when he was granted permission by Pope Innocent III to expand his ministry into Muslim territory.[20, 21]

PART TWO
The Missionary

"He did not hesitate to go to Egypt and there bravely to appear in the very presence of the Sultan. In the annals of the Church, too, are not the names of those numerous apostles of the Gospel who, from the beginning, that is to say, in the springtime of the Order of Minors, found martyrdom in Syria and Morocco, recorded in words of highest praise? With the passing of time this apostolate had been developed with much zeal and often with great shedding of blood by the numerous Franciscan brotherhood, for many lands inhabited by the heathen have been entrusted to their care through the express commands of the Roman Pontiffs."

—Pope Pius XI, *Rite Expiatis*, no. 37.*

---

* http://www.vatican.va/holy_father/pius_xi/encyclicals/documents/hf_p-xi_enc_30041926_rite-expiatis_en.html.

Chapter 8

Missionary Journey to The Middle East

IS heart on fire with the love of God, Francis was eager to preach the saving word of Christ, heeding the counsel of St. Paul: "Preach the word: be instant in season, out of season: reprove, entreat, rebuke in all patience and doctrine." (*2 Timothy* 4:2). Fully aware of the dangers, Francis was determined to go on a mission to the unbelievers of the Muslim nations. The primary sources are in agreement that he was now ready to sacrifice his life and die for Christ,[1] so there can be little doubt that the intent of his journey was to preach the Gospel even at the risk of martyrdom. It was with this disposition and outlook that St. Francis, with one companion, set out in the second half of 1212 to reach the Middle East.[2]

From the port of Ancona in Italy, the pair boarded a ship bound for the Levant, the eastern shores of the Mediterranean, and set sail on the Adriatic Sea. They were headed for Syria, to preach the Gospel to the Muslims. However, they had barely started their journey when unfavorable winds arose, turning the boat in the direction of the Dalmatian coast on the opposite shores of the Adriatic from the Italian peninsula. There the ship's voyage abruptly terminated, and the disappointed friars disembarked. Realizing it would be difficult to find anther ship headed for the Middle East, Francis and his companion decided to return to their homeland.

43

Although they were successful in their search for a boat bound for Ancona, they were refused passage because they were unable to pay their way. Undaunted and desperate, and trusting that the merciful God would look kindly on their actions, the two friars clandestinely stowed away on the vessel.[3] A compassionate shipmate who knew of their plight arranged to have food and water secretly provided to the stowaway friars. An anecdote reported by Celano relates that the ship soon became bogged down in a storm lasting many days, and the sailors ran out of food. However, a portion of the provisions that had been given covertly to Francis and his companion still remained. "These, by divine grace and power, were multiplied."[4] And so, through a miracle reminiscent of the multiplication of the loaves and fishes, Our Lord's faithful Franciscans were able to sustain everyone on board during the remaining days of the voyage!

Approximately a year later, in 1213, Francis risked martyrdom for the second time, in the hope of preaching the Gospel to those who had not yet accepted the Good News. His goal was to reach Morocco, in order to evangelize and convert Sheik Miramolino Mohammed al-Nasir and his followers.[5] But this time he made the journey by land. Along with one friar who accompanied him, Francis trekked northwest from the Apennines of central Italy, skirted the Maritime Alps, and crossed into southernmost France. St. Bonaventure reports that the great enthusiasm of Francis often caused him to leave his companion far behind, so eager was he to bring Christ to the unbelievers. The condition of his physical health, however, did not match the strength of his spirit. Shortly after crossing the Spanish frontier, he fell prey to a prolonged illness, and was forced to retrace his steps. The Lord, it seemed, wished Francis back in Italy to nurture the young Order he had founded, "and so he returned to tend the flock which had been committed to his care."[6]

That same year, Pope Innocent III initiated plans for a Fifth Crusade, which was finally launched by his successor, Pope Honorius III, in 1217. Its aim of retaking the Holy Land and Jerusalem was to be accomplished by first seizing control of the Muslim nation of Egypt, ruled by Sultan al-Malik al-Kamil. The third and final attempt by St. Francis to reach the Middle East took place during the Fifth Crusade. This time, he would arrive in Muslim territory and succeed in preaching the word of God to the Sultan and his court.

That his visit took place during the Fifth Crusade cannot be doubted, since it is well documented by historians and chroniclers of the era, both secular and Franciscan, although Arabic sources are lacking. The following narration of his sojourn in the Middle East is derived primarily from thirteenth-century Franciscan sources and contemporary accounts. The integral story and its main components will be related in a straightforward fashion, relying on these early records, and some later historical studies.

Francis undertook this missionary expedition in 1219, after the Crusade was well underway. The prelude to this voyage had occurred two years earlier, when in May of 1217 Francis had convoked the first General Chapter of the Friars Minor. At this seminal Chapter, the Order divided the territories that they would evangelize into about a dozen districts, seven of which were in Italy. The districts were formally called "Provinces," and Provincial Ministers were appointed to administer them, along with groups of volunteer friars.

Francis took a personal interest in the establishment of the missionary Province designated for the Middle East, the Franciscan Province of Syria. He chose the port city of St. John of Acre in Palestine as headquarters for this Syrian Province. At that time the Province extended all along the Mediterranean eastern coast from Egypt to Greece, and most importantly, it included the Holy Land.[7] The historical significance of this Franciscan outreach was momentous. In fact, a little over one hundred years after Francis' death, Pope Clement VI formally entrusted the Christian shrines of the Holy Land to the custody of the Order of Friars Minor, as a just reward for their sacrifices. In spite of difficulties and setbacks through the centuries, the Franciscans have maintained their presence in the Middle East to this day. "The Custody of the Holy Places, maintained in perpetual peril of death, constitutes the greatest glory of the Franciscan Order."[8]

To administer the Syrian Province based at St. John of Acre, St. Francis appointed Brother Elias of Cortona, one of his ablest followers. This same Brother Elias was later chosen by Francis to be the second Minister General of the Order, succeeding Peter of Catania. A controversial figure, Elias later in his life was excommunicated by the Pope because of disobedience. He died repentant, although no longer a member of the Order.[9] Ironically, he is the person considered most responsible for the construction of the great Basilica of St. Francis in Assisi.

With a Franciscan presence now established in the Middle East, the Saint set out on his third attempt to reach the area, leaving on June 24, 1219, which was the Feast of St. John the Baptist—a saint who figures prominently in subsequent events. Most likely, Francis once again embarked from the Italian port of Ancona, but this time on one of the galleys comprising the Crusader fleet. A large number of the brothers had accompanied him to the port, but he chose only twelve to go with him, by means of a resourceful tactic. Francis asked a young child who was present at the docks to point out at random a dozen friars—a method which hopefully indicated God's choice as to who should go, and also insured that no one would feel slighted by favoritism.

The names of five of the twelve are known: Sabatino and Barbaro, who were two of St. Francis' earliest companions, Leonardo di Gislerio, Brother Illuminato d'Arce, and Pietro of Cattanio (Peter of Catania).[10] Peter was one of the original twelve followers of Francis—in fact, he was the second after Bernard, and would be appointed by him to be the first Minister General of the Order. Not much is known about Brother Illuminato (or Illuminatus), other than his being placed by Dante in a heavenly sphere of his *Paradiso:*[11]

Illuminato here, And Agostino join me: two they were,
Among the first of those barefooted meek ones,
Who sought God's friendship in the cord. . .

However, this brother is very important in the context of St. Francis' mission to the Middle East. Much of what is known about the activities and exploits of Francis on this expedition was obtained from information related by Brother Illuminato to the great Franciscan scholar and historian St. Bonaventure.[12, 13]

In July, the Crusader vessel bearing the Saint and his twelve companions arrived at the port of St. John of Acre, located almost at the mid-point along the Palestinian-Syrian coast bordering the Mediterranean. Today the city is known as "Atta" or "Atto" and is part of modern-day Israel. Situated on the northern arm of the Bay of Haifa, it is no longer the major port it once was in medieval times. St. John of Acre was not the final goal of the Crusader fleet, since the Christian force was headed for Damietta in Egypt in order to aid in the siege of that city. However, Francis disembarked at St. John of Acre in order to visit the first Province of his Order in the Middle East.

Little information exists in Franciscan sources regarding the Saint's visit to his overseas Province of Syria in 1219.

Here he would have met Brother Elias of Cortona, who was
the Administrator, Caesar of Speyer (or Spires), and any of
the brethren who had volunteered to serve in the Province.
He did not remain long in St. John of Acre, and before July
was over, he resumed his passage to the Egyptian port of
Damietta on board another Crusader vessel. Of the original
twelve voyagers, only Peter of Catania and Illuminato stayed
with Francis; the others were sent by him to various parts of
the Province. Joining him on this leg of the journey were
some of the friars who had been in residence at the Syrian
Province, including Caesar of Speyer and Brother Elias.[14]
Caesar of Speyer would later be given the responsibility for
administering the first Province of the Order in Germany.

Chapter 9

The Tragic Battle
of Damietta

THE city of Damietta, Egypt, was originally situated close to the Mediterranean coast on the Nile River delta, at one of the branches of that great river. It was the gateway to Cairo and thus strategically important militarily. A major port in ancient times, the city was still an active commercial center during the Middle Ages. However, due to its vulnerability to attacks, the city was razed about fifty years after Francis appeared there and was rebuilt further inland. Consequently, the modern city is now about eight miles from the Mediterranean Sea and sits on the east bank of a branch of the Nile.[1]

The leader of the Crusader army at Damietta was John of Brienne, the King of Jerusalem. This title was largely symbolic, since most of the Latin Kingdom of Jerusalem, which had been established after the First Crusade, had been lost to the Muslims, including the Holy City itself. Prior to his conversion, Francis had attempted to become a knight in the service of Walter of Brienne, John's brother. His intention had been to join Walter's army, which was fighting in southern Italy on behalf of Pope Innocent III, against troops loyal to Emperor Frederick II. Francis had outfitted himself with elaborate and expensive armor, but after a series of dreams, he understood that knighthood, soldiery and bearing arms were not to be his calling. Ironically, years later, he was finally accompanying a Christian army of knights led by a Brienne, but this time as a spiritual warrior in the service of Christ. By the end of July 1219, Francis and his small group of friars stood before the walls of Damietta near the Nile delta, mingling among the ranks of the Crusaders. The army was eager for the taste of battle, and was becoming impatient with their prolonged siege of the fortified town. The enthusiasm of the soldiers encircling Damietta was ignited by various motives, ranging from a heroic desire for the glory of Christ and Christendom, to base greed for the spoils of war. They nourished their excitement by harkening to colorful legends and rumors. One such tale held that it was at this branch of the Nile that Moses was found floating in a basket; also, according to legend, the area was the birthplace of the prophet Jeremias.[2] In addition, a prophetic book written in Arabic and circulating in the Crusader camp foretold that "a watery city in Egypt" would be captured by Christians. The prophecy served only to increase the thirst for battle among many of the knights. The army took it to be a prediction of the taking of Damietta and of the ultimate defeat of the Saracen army in Egypt.[3, 4]

Plans had been afoot in the camp to mount a decisive offensive against the city's determined Muslim inhabitants, who had successfully defended Damietta during the year-long siege. If the city fell, it would lead to the taking of Cairo and thus to the fall of all Egypt. Unfortunately, by mid-summer the Crusader fleet could no longer approach close enough to Damietta to mount an attack, because the river had sunk too low.[5] Pressure then began to build within the rank and file of the Christian army to take some kind of action, especially since their leaders had refused until now to attack the main Muslim force, which was personally led by the Muslim king, Sultan al-Kamil. His army, encamped further up the Nile at al-Fariskur, was trying to break the siege of Damietta in order to relieve the city. After much deliberation, the Crusaders determined to launch an all-out attack by land and sea on the camp of the Sultan, instead of marching on Damietta itself. The battle was planned for the 29th of August.[6, 7] By the time the eve of the battle arrived, Francis had been living alongside the Crusader army for about a month, and was quite aware of their capabilities and shortcomings. The night before the attack found him deeply absorbed in prayer.[8] By morning he had received a clear prophetic insight that a clash that day against the forces of the Sultan would be a disaster for the Christians. He desperately wanted to inform the Crusaders of this revelation, but was put off by the intense enthusiasm of the troops, who were clamoring for the thrill of combat.

In Bonaventure's *Major Life* of the Saint, Francis is quoted as asking one of his companions if he should nonetheless make his prophecy known to the soldiers, by informing them that if they went into battle that day, victory would not be theirs. "But if I say that, they will say I am a fool. And if I do not say it, my conscience will give me no rest. What do you think I should do?" His enlightened companion, who in all likelihood was Illuminato, wisely replied: "Brother, do not worry about being criticized. This will not be the first time you were called a fool. Obey your conscience and have more regard for God than for human beings."[9] This incident clearly demonstrated the humility of St. Francis, who sought the counsel of one of his own followers before deciding on a course of action. One can reasonably surmise that he knew before-hand what he must do, but perhaps he wished to share his own thoughts and concerns, or sought to test the insight of his companion.

Without further hesitation, Francis resolutely approached the Crusaders and made known his apprehension about the outcome of the looming conflict. He pleaded with the Papal Legate Cardinal Pelagius, with John of Brienne, and with the military commanders, all men who greatly respected his counsel. He exhorted them to suspend the battle, warning them that they would lose if they chose openly to attack the Sultan's army that day. While the leaders were swayed by his entreaties and considered revoking the order, Francis had less success in persuading the rank and file soldiers. True to his premonition, they scorned his words of warning, contending that it would be a joke for the knights to take advice from this lowly man of the cloth, and shabby cloth at that. Almost spitefully, they become more determined than ever to join the battle, hardening their hearts. Seeing the anger of their men and fearing to be considered cowards, the commanders felt they had no alternative but to proceed with their original plans for the attack.

Thus on August 29, 1219, the Christians moved by land and sea against the Muslim camp. It was the feast of the beheading of St. John the Baptist, an ominous portent. Francis, knowing what the outcome would be, was unwilling to watch the clash with his own eyes. Three separate times, he bid one of his friars to go and watch the battle and report back on its progress.[10]

The Saracens had led the knights into a trap by feigning to flee, drawing the Crusaders into an area where there was no water available for themselves or their horses. Drinking water was crucial in providing relief from the hot Egyptian mid-summer sun. The out-maneuvered Christian leaders debated possible strategies, while the Sultan's army remained in a holding position. As the day grew hotter, disorder within the ranks of the Crusaders grew, since many of the men had become feverish and disoriented from the parching heat and lack of water. Suddenly, the Muslims, aware of the confusion of their enemies, attacked on one flank, spreading panic among the cornered Christians. Many simply fled the battlefield, and others, driven in part by thirst, leaped into the Nile.[11] Radulfus, the Latin Patriarch of Jerusalem, had carried a relic of the True Cross into the battle. As he witnessed the rout of the army, he stood his ground and raised the sacred relic in the face of the fleeing Crusaders, beseeching them to stand their ground—as some in fact did. Most of these were grouped around John of Brienne, who fought brilliantly. But in spite of a valiant effort, particularly by the Knights Templar, the Hospitallers, some French and Germans, and the Pisans, the Crusader army was forced to retreat. The Muslim forces advanced to the edge of the moat that protected the Crusader base camp itself, before breaking off the attack. Not only did the Christians suffer heavy losses, but many nobles were captured, including the bishop-elect of Beauvais.[12] In the end, the result was a tragic rout of the Christian army, with over five thousand killed and another thousand taken prisoner. Survivors blamed the defeat on the burning hot sun and their extreme thirst, which had sapped the fighting prowess of the knights.

By sunset on this feast of the beheading of St. John the Baptist, the Crusaders were mourning their losses with anguished desperation. Francis was especially grieved at the near annihilation of the Spanish contingents, which had been the most impetuous in joining the battle, with the result that very few survived.[13] Adding to the grief was the discovery that a great many of the Crusaders had been beheaded by the enemy. This horror befell about fifty horsemen of the Knights Templar, thirty of the Germans, and over twenty Hospitallers. One chronicler of the battle wrote that John the Baptist found many companions that day. This great Saint, who was decapitated because of his love for God, was joined by scores of fallen Crusaders, whose own faith in

Christ had led them to the same fate.[14]

Francis' biographer Celano surmised that the Crusaders had lost because they had defied the will of God by ignoring the friar's admonition. He wrote: "But if victory is to be hoped for from on high, battles must be entrusted to the Spirit of God."[15] St. Bonaventure noted that this was a case where "the wisdom of a beggar was not to be scorned."[16] He also cited the Scripture verse: "The soul of a holy man discovereth sometimes true things, more than seven watchmen that sit in a high place to watch." (*Ecclesiasticus* 37:18). At least one contemporary pointedly stated that the defeat was in fact a just punishment from on High, since the army had ignored the warnings of Francis, following their own emotions and thirst for battle rather than fearing God.[17]

An area of contention among scholars to this day is whether Francis' preaching against launching the attack indicated that he was opposed to this Fifth Crusade as a whole. Those who feel that the Crusades were an unjust attempt to regain the Holy Land would certainly be pleased to enroll the great Saint of Assisi among their number. However, it can only be said for certain that his pleadings to avoid fighting the Muslims referred to this particular battle on this particular day. Further, it is evident that he was against this confrontation only because he had learned in prayer that the Christians would lose the clash—and even then he was hesitant at first to make his protest. By implication, then, if he had not received this revelation, he would have made no objection to their going into battle that day.

One cannot reasonably conclude from the ancient sources that Francis was opposed not just to this encounter, but also to the entire Crusade. In fact, even one modern historian notes that "unreserved support of the Crusade had become normative in the Order."[18] In addition, as will be seen in a subsequent chapter, St. Francis made it clear during his discourse with the Sultan that he believed the Crusade itself was justified.*

---

* The entire historical episode of the Crusades (11th through 13th centuries) against the Muslim forces in and about the Holy Land is almost universally misunderstood by people today. The Catholic historian and historical commentator, Hilaire Belloc (1870-1953), has perhaps best explained the root cause of the Crusades. They were due to the Muslim attacks on the Eastern Roman Empire, under the Roman government at Constantinople (which finally fell to the Turks in 1453). Belloc maintains that the Roman Empire in the West never actually "fell," as most history texts would have it, dating this "fall" at 476 A.D., when Rome in the West failed to select a new Emperor. Belloc maintains that there was no single force big enough during Rome's history to defeat it entirely—though portions of the Empire in the West were whittled away. Rather, the Empire in the West grew old and changed, and the government from Rome, and later from Ravenna, was no longer effectively able to manage it. Yet the people of the Empire still considered themselves part of that Empire, a fact illustrated in the year 800, when Charlemagne was crowned Holy Roman Emperor at Rome. Why would he call his realm by this name unless he and his people believed the Empire still existed? In the 6th century, Islam had exploded out of Arabia, taken all of North Africa, and by the first third of the 8th century had conquered Spain. Its advance in Europe was halted in central France in 732 when the forces of Charles Martel defeated the Muslim army at Tours, after which they retired behind the Pyrenees Mountains in Spain. Then when the Turks were converted to Islam and the entire Islamic holy wars were renewed during the 10th Century in the Holy Land and Middle East—an area under the Eastern Roman Empire— the people of the West (with all this history well in mind) rose up in the form of the Crusades, or a holy war against Islam, finally in order *to come to the aid of the Eastern portion of THEIR EMPIRE*—which for the past 1,000 years had controlled the Middle East! In this light, the Crusades make great sense, especially when one realizes that the Christians of the Roman Empire had been battling Islam for more than 500 years when the First Crusade was launched.—*Publisher*, 2007.

Chapter 10

Face to Face with the Sultan

BY the marvelous working of Divine Providence, it was the very defeat of the Christians at Damietta that gave Francis the opportunity he had been seeking for so long: that is, to speak to the Muslims face to face about Christ, despite the risk of martyrdom. Their leader, Sultan al-Malik al-Kamil, was one of the most important Islamic potentates of the time, since he was the ruler of Egypt, Palestine, and Syria. It was this sultan, operating out of his nearby encampment, who was personally in charge of the defense of Damietta, and who had just routed the Christian army.

However, al-Kamil realized that reinforcements from Europe could arrive at any moment to buttress the Crusader forces. He was also aware that the Muslim inhabitants of the city had been greatly weakened by starvation and illness, due to the prolonged siege. In addition, the Nile had failed to overflow and irrigate the coastal croplands, so a general famine throughout Egypt was feared.[1] Thus, rather than marching forward to rout completely the remaining knights after their ignominious defeat, he sent one of his Christian prisoners to their camp with the offer of a temporary truce. The offer was accepted, and hostilities ceased for most of the month of September, 1219.

Taking advantage of the pause in the fighting, Francis approached the Papal Legate, Cardinal Pelagius of Albano. The Poverello requested permission to cross the lines separating the opposing armies, in order to bring the Gospel of peace to the Muslim leaders.*

Although the Sultan's men would have allowed official representatives of the Crusader army to cross their lines during the truce negotiations, a person in Christian religious garb wandering toward the Muslim camp would be in great danger. The Legate Pelagius feared that Francis might even be killed, since at one time al-Kamil reportedly avowed that "anyone who brought him the head of a Christian should be awarded with a Byzantine gold piece."[2] Thus, the Legate at first refused to grant permission for Francis to cross over; but the friar's persistence and fearlessness led him to reverse his decision, and he agreed to allow Francis and one companion to proceed.[3] This is an excellent example of the obedience and loyalty of the Saint to the authority of the Church. If Pelagius had not been with the Crusaders, Francis might have gone on his own initiative to attempt to convert the Sultan. But with the Papal Legate present, Francis was prepared to submit his own inclination to the decision of the Church, which for him reflected the will of God.

St. Bonaventure reports that Francis' companion was Brother Illuminato,[4] as does Butler in his *Lives of the Saints,* apparently taking Bonaventure as his source.[5] In fact, as mentioned previously, Bonaventure's account of Francis at Damietta is apparently based on the personal testimony of Brother Illuminato—a strong indication that it was he who accompanied Francis. This loyal follower had been with him since 1210, almost a decade, and would survive his mentor by forty years.[6]

The Bishop of Acre, Jacques de Vitry, who was with the Crusader army, described his impressions of Francis' courage:

---

* A minority of scholars place Francis' visit as taking place some months later, after the fall of Damietta to the Crusaders; however, at that juncture there was no period of truce.

> We saw Brother Francis, the founder of the Order of
> the Friars Minor, a simple and unlearned man,
> though very amiable and beloved by God and man,
> who was respected universally. He came to the Chris-
> tian army, which was lying before Damietta, and an
> excess of fervor had such an effect upon him, that,
> protected solely by the shield of faith, he had the dar-
> ing to go to the Sultan's camp to preach to him and to
> his subjects the faith of Jesus Christ.[7]

As the two friars set out, they came across a pair of
lambs grazing in the fields which separated the opposing
armies. This fortuitous encounter filled Francis with joy
and confidence—he saw in the gentle creatures a reflection
of himself and his companion, as they embarked on their
peaceful mission to the enemy camp. He urged Illuminato
to have complete trust in God's protection, since the two
lambs made him mindful of the Scripture, "Behold I send
you as sheep in the midst of wolves. Be ye therefore wise
as serpents and simple as doves." (*Matthew* 10:16). And
wolves they would encounter, justifying the apprehension
of the Papal Legate.

The early documents are unanimous in agreeing that the
two Franciscans were subjected to rough treatment upon
crossing into Muslim territory. The men of God were seized
in a violent manner by the sentries, assaulted, and bound in
chains. Celano reports that Francis "was captured by the
Sultan's soldiers, was insulted and beaten" yet showed no
fear even when threatened with torture and death.[8] The two
friars repeatedly shouted out to their captors the word for
"Sultan," to try to communicate their intention of seeing
him. The battered men were then "dragged before the Sultan
by God's providence, just as Francis wished."[9] Jacques de
Vitry wrote that "The Saracens arrested him on his way,"

after Francis told the Muslim sentinels that he was a Christian and wished to see their master.[10] The prisoners were hauled into the opulent war tent of Sultan al-Kamil, who demanded of them the reason for their coming. Were they messengers sent by the Crusaders, or did they seek to convert to Islam? The poor man of Assisi stood fearlessly before the Sultan, who was seated amid his regal trappings of power. The lowly Poverello faced his inquisitor with complete confidence in God, mindful of the words of Scripture: "And when they shall bring you into the synagogues, and to magistrates and powers, be not solicitous how or what you shall answer, or what you shall say; for the Holy Ghost shall teach you in the same hour what you must say." (*Luke* 12:11-12). These prophetic words of Our Lord were fulfilled in His follower Francis that day, as the humble friar resolutely confronted the powerful Sultan.

With Illuminato probably acting as interpreter,[11] Francis boldly replied that yes, they were in fact messengers. But, he explained, he and his companion had been sent by God and not by man. Francis began at once to proclaim to the Sultan the Gospel message of salvation, declaring Jesus Christ as both Saviour and true God made man. Perhaps most importantly, as it turned out, Francis announced that his personal concern was for the eternal salvation of the soul of al-Kamil.[12] The Sultan listened intently while Francis preached the Faith to him and his attendants. As he witnessed the Saint's courage, enthusiasm and steadfastness, he became deeply moved. Vitry described the Sultan's transformation: " . . . that cruel beast, became sweetness itself . . ."[13]

The response of Sultan al-Kamil while listening to Francis, contrasted remarkably with the way his own sentinels and soldiers had greeted the Franciscans. The Sultan, impressed by the courage and spirituality of this inspired speaker, wished to hear more. The wolf had been trans-

formed into a lamb,[14] thanks to the influence of the Saint on
the educated and open-minded Sultan. One modern thesis
proposes that al-Kamil was being attentive to this teaching
of the Koran: "Nearest among them in love to the believers
wilt thou find those who say, 'We are Christians': because
amongst these are men devoted to learning and men who
have renounced the world, and they are not arrogant."
(*Koran* 5: 82).[15, 16]

Francis did not directly attack the religion of Mohammed,
but under the guidance of the Holy Spirit, continued to
expound the truths of the Christian religion. Celano rhetor-
ically asks whether anyone can possibly narrate Francis'
steadfastness. "With what strength of spirit he spoke to him,
with what eloquence and confidence he replied to those who
insulted the Christian law."[17] To Bonaventure, the zeal of
Francis reflected the Gospel promise: "For I will give you a
mouth and wisdom, which all your adversaries shall not be
able to resist and gainsay."[18] (*Luke* 21:15).

An early font presents the following account of the discourse of the Franciscans: "If you do not wish to believe," said
the two friars, "we will commend your soul to God, because
we declare that if you die while holding to your law, you will
be lost; God will not accept your soul. For this reason we
have come to you."[19] They added that they would demonstrate to the Sultan's wisest counselors the truth of Christianity, before which Mohammed's law counted for nothing.[20]
In answer to this challenge, and in order to confute the
teaching of the two missionaries, the Sultan called in his
religious advisers, the *imams*. However, they refused to dispute with the Christians and instead insisted that they be
killed, in accordance with Islamic law.[21, 22]

But the Sultan, captivated by the speech of the two Franciscans, and by their sincere concern for his own eternal
salvation, ignored the demand of his courtiers. Instead,

al-Kamil listened willingly to Francis, permitting him great liberty in his preaching. He told his *imams* that beheading the friars would be an unjust recompense for their efforts, since they had arrived with the praiseworthy intention of seeking his personal salvation.[23] To Francis he said: "I am going to go counter to what my religious advisors demand and will not cut off your heads . . . you have risked your own lives in order to save my soul."[24]

The two Franciscans were guests of the Sultan for a number of days, since al-Kamil enjoyed having Francis with him, and "sent for him in particular."[25] He seemed preoccupied with them and made certain that the wounds they had received from his sentinels were tended to. He also saw to it that treatment was given for Francis' eyes.[26] His existing eye problems had been aggravated by the Egyptian sun and the arid, dusty environment, causing him to contract an eye disease which would persist until his death.[27]

Vitry mentions in his writings that the Muslim leader "kept him with him for a few days and with a great deal of attention listened to him."[28] Francis in turn must have been quite encouraged by the sympathetic attitude of the Sultan. He realized that his preaching was having at least some effect, since at one point the Muslim leader told the friar, "I believe that your faith is good and true." Such was the recollection of Francis' companion, Brother Illuminato, in his interviews with St. Bonaventure.[29]

While it might seem unusual that a Muslim potentate should be so attracted to Christianity, one has to consider the merits and person of this bearer of the Gospel message to the Egyptian. Francis was one of the most charismatic and remarkable Saints in the history of the Church. The Sultan's receptivity and courtesy, upon seeing that Francis was a just man, seem to have been influenced by this advice from the *Koran*: "And do not dispute with the followers of the

Book, except by what is best, except those of them who act unjustly." (*Koran* 29: 46).[30, 31]

In addition, the Sultan, who was a cultured person with a poetic bent, was undoubtedly well acquainted with the Muslim Sufi mystics. Sources indicate that al-Kamil's closest spiritual teacher was the Sufi al-Fakhr al-Farisi, on whose tombstone is mentioned the Sufi's adventure with al-Kamil and "that which befalls him because of the monk." This, incidentally, is the only known Arabic writing alluding to Francis' visit.[32]

The Sufis were ascetics who bore some striking similarities to the early Franciscans. They wore coarse robes girded with a cord and were itinerants who sought alms. They embraced a philosophy which held that a true Sufi possessed nothing and was himself possessed by nothing, an outlook quite similar, in some respects, to the Franciscan emphasis on total poverty.[33] Further, the thirteenth century is considered the Sufi "golden age," the period when Sufism had its greatest flowering in the Muslim world.[34] It is quite possible, then, that the Sultan's curiosity and interest in St. Francis, and the hospitality that he showed him, could have been influenced by the remarkable similarities between this mendicant follower of Christ and the wandering Muslim Sufis.

Perhaps, an additional cause for the benign reception accorded Francis was that the Muslim leader saw in Francis a useful ally in the ongoing negotiations with the Crusaders.[35] Although he had just handed the Christian army a crushing defeat, he had many reasons to wish for an end to the war, as previously mentioned.

Even though Francis had not been actually sent as an official truce emissary to the Sultan, in reality his was the true "peace mission" to the Muslim camp—in the sense of bringing the peace of Christ to the Islamic leaders. Such a mission would come to fruition if they were to accept Christianity.

Converting the Muslims by his preaching was the ultimate goal of Francis' efforts, and a peaceful end to the war would be a consequence of their conversion. In the words of scholar Christoph Maier, "Francis, like the crusaders, wanted to liberate the holy places in Palestine from Muslim rule. What was different was his strategy . . . He wanted their total submission to the Christian faith."[36]

Chapter 11

Trial by Fire

O N fire with the Holy Spirit, Francis joyfully proclaimed Christ to the Islamic Sultan and his court. He even offered to endure the painful flames of an actual fire, in order to prove the truth of his teaching. The sovereign had been insisting that Francis prolong his stay, and the Saint replied that he would gladly continue to remain with him for love of God, provided that the Muslim leader and his people would convert to Christianity. The Sultan responded by renewing the earlier proposal, that is, that his *imams* and philosophers discuss with the friars the relative merits of the two religions. But this time it was Francis who declined, replying, "Our faith is greater than human reason. Reason is of no use unless a person believes."[1] Instead, in order to prove the truth of the Christian Faith, Francis challenged the Sultan to ascertain which religion was "more sure and more holy" by having a fire kindled. Then the Sultan should bid these same *imams* and philosophers to enter the conflagration along with Francis, to see who would emerge unharmed by the flames.*

The Sultan's response was a polite refusal, joined with the frank admission that he did not believe his religious leaders would be willing to face the possibility of affliction or death in order to demonstrate the truth of their beliefs.

---

* Trial by ordeal, also known as *ordalia*, was a common practice in ancient and medieval times to determine the guilt or innocence of an accused person.

St. Bonaventure adds the aside that the Sultan saw one of his eldest and most respected *imams* slip away upon hearing Francis' proposition.[2]

Seeing that the Saracens would not submit to such a contest, Francis then offered to enter the fire unaccompanied. If the fire harmed him, they must attribute this to his sins alone. But should he emerge from the flames unscathed, the Sultan and his court must agree to convert to the Christian Religion, acknowledging the power and wisdom of Christ as Lord and Saviour of all. Once again the ruler refused the challenge, saying he feared his followers would revolt if he should renounce his own religion. "I could never do that. My people would stone me."[3] Since he was the ruler of the Islamic territories of Egypt, Syria, and the Holy Land, news of the conversion of the Sultan and any of his men to Christianity would indeed have quickly reverberated throughout the Middle East, with ominous consequences for them.

Challenged by the willingness of Francis to submit to a testing of his faith, al-Kamil devised a clever plan to draw the friar into a situation where he would be forced to choose between two alternatives. One of the choices would show contempt for his Islamic host and court, and the other would be disrespectful of his own Christian religion. It was a ploy similar to that of those who wished to entrap Jesus by asking Him if it was lawful to pay tribute to Caesar, expecting that whether He responded with a yes or a no, they would be able to condemn Him either way.

The Sultan had in his possession an elaborate multi-colored carpet that was decorated with cross-shaped motifs, and he commanded his men to lay it out before him. He boasted to his followers that if Francis approached him by stepping on the crosses as he walked upon the carpet, he would accuse him of being guilty of insulting his Lord. On the other hand, if he refused to walk upon the rug, declining to draw near to the Sultan himself, he would be guilty of insolence and disrespect to his host.

Francis was then summoned to appear before al-Kamil. Without hesitation, he walked upon the rug and traversed its entire length in order to greet his host. He was fully aware of treading on the crosses, but, as Brother Illuminato later commented, Francis "received his instructions for his actions as well as for his words from the very plenitude of God."[4]

The Sultan gloated as he accused Francis of insulting his own God by stepping on the crosses woven into the carpet. He charged him with trampling underfoot the very sign of that Saviour whom Christians adore. But Francis surprised the Sultan by denying that he had walked over the sign of the cross of Christ. "Thieves were also crucified with Our Lord," he explained. We Christians have the True Cross, which we do venerate with great devotion, he continued. But if we have the True Cross, then that which has been left to you are the crosses of the thieves. "That is why I had no scruple in walking over the symbols of brigands."[5]

God had inspired Francis to view the crosses on the unbelieving Sultan's carpet to be the gibbets of the men who were crucified with Christ. The Saint had artfully dodged the sovereign's ruse by differentiating the crosses that had been used to punish the votaries of the world from the True Cross upon which Jesus hung—just as Christ had evaded the snare of the Pharisees by making a distinction between the things that belong to Caesar and those that are of God: "And Jesus answering, said to them: Render therefore to Caesar the things that are Caesar's, and to God the things that are God's. And they marvelled at him." (*Mark* 12: 17-18).

Francis is also reported to have said to the Sultan: "Nothing of the sacred cross of the Saviour belongs to you or is amongst you."[6] With the words "amongst you," Francis was alluding to an ongoing controversy between the Christians and Muslims about the True Cross. A relic of the Cross, carried by the Latin Patriarch of Jerusalem, was in fact venerated in the Crusader camp that was then besieging Damietta.[7] However, during the truce negotiations with the Christians, al-Kamil had alleged that he himself was in possession of the largest existing remnant of the True Cross, which had been captured by the Muslims in the battle of Hattin in 1187.[8]

The Christian forces, however, were not convinced that the Sultan had this sacred relic in his possession, since it was rumored that the Muslims had lost it shortly after the battle of Hattin. Francis' assertions that the "cross of the thieves" was the Sultan's portion and that the True Cross was not "amongst you" was probably a veiled challenge to the Muslim leader to prove that he actually had a relic of Christ's cross in his custody. At any rate the truth was not to be known, since the peace talks eventually broke down and the battle of Damietta was resumed. Much later, after the Crusaders had ultimately lost the Fifth Crusade, surrender terms included the return of the Muslim's portion of the True Cross. However, al-Kamil was never able to locate it, and this part of the sacred relic was never found again.[9]

The story of the "carpet with crosses" inspired a modern-day Franciscan, Fr. Christopher Rengers, O.F.M. Cap. to compose this refrain:[10]

Help Us Tread On Sin

To trap the friars, the Sultan had a scheme:
A carpet with crosses before the Sultan spread.
Would they refuse, or on the carpet tread?
To refuse would to the Sultan insult seem.
To walk on the cross would Christ Himself blaspheme.

Then Francis walked on the carpet for all to see.
The Sultan exclaimed: "Do you not Christ offend?"
"Not so, before His cross my knee I bend
On Calvary's hill the crosses numbered three.
To tread on crosses of thieves I haste with glee.
Saint Francis, send us friars of skill
To help us know the Father's will.
Whose words enlighten and amuse,
And plans of dark design confuse.
Saint Francis, help us tread on sin.
Take up our cross and heaven win.

Al-Kamil made another attempt to test St. Francis, this
time in the matter of the Gospel teachings of Christ. This
incident shows that he had some familiarity with Christian
doctrine, perhaps based on what had already been preached
to him by Francis. The Sultan confronted the friar with the
words from Jesus' Sermon on the Mount, recounted in the
Gospel of St. Matthew: "But I say to you not to resist evil: but
if one strike thee on thy right cheek, turn to him also the
other: And if a man will contend with thee in judgment, and
take away thy coat, let go thy cloak also unto him." (*Matthew*
5: 39-40).

The Sultan asked Francis why, in light of this teaching of
Jesus, Crusaders should be invading the lands of the Muslims? Since the passage teaches "turning the other cheek"
and repaying evil with good, the Sultan was contending that
there was no justification for the Crusader invasions, even
though he knew that the Muslims had taken the land by
force from the Christians centuries earlier.

Once again the response of Francis surprised al-Kamil.
The Saint declared that the Sultan had not completely stud-
ied the Gospel, and pointed out to the King the words Our
Lord had spoken earlier in the same discourse:

And if thy right eye scandalize thee, pluck it out and
cast it from thee. For it is expedient for thee that one
of thy members should perish, rather than that thy
whole body be cast into hell. And if thy right hand
scandalize thee, cut it off, and cast it from thee: for it
is expedient for thee that one of thy members should
perish, rather than that thy whole body go into hell."
(*Matthew* 5: 29-30).

Francis then proceeded to impart a distinctive interpretation to these lines, by referring them to those who attempt to
turn Christians away from their faith and love of God. The
Sultan was as dear to him as his own eye, he admitted to the
potentate.[11] But, explaining Our Lord's words that a person
should pluck out his own eye if it is leading him astray, Francis continued.

Here he wanted to teach us that every man, however
dear and close he is to us, and even if he is as precious
to us as the apple of our eye, must be repulsed, pulled
out, expelled if he seeks to turn us aside from the
faith and love of our God. That is why it is just that
Christians invade the land you inhabit, for you blaspheme the name of Christ and alienate everyone you
can from His worship. But if you were to recognize,
confess, and adore the Creator and Redeemer, Christians would love you as themselves . . .[12]

When Francis had finished addressing the Sultan, "All the
spectators were in admiration at his answers."[13]
    Al-Kamil, by citing the Scripture teaching that one should
repay evil with good, was in effect stating that the Christians should repay some evil committed by the Muslims with
a good action on their part, or by turning the other cheek.

With these words the Sultan was in point of fact condemning himself. He was inferring that he and his people were in fact evildoers, and that the Christians should not have repaid evil for evil by fighting them in this Crusade. One has to wonder what iniquity he could be attributing to his own people in the light of the ongoing war, if not the centuries-old Muslim conquest and occupation of lands, peoples and nations that had once been primarily Christian?

In addition, Francis' rebuke of the Sultan makes it clear that he was not opposed to the Crusade, because he saw it as a justified attempt to retake those countries that had been lost to the Muslim armies. One of the foremost experts on Francis and the Fifth Crusade, James M. Powell, asserts: "Francis of Assisi went to Damietta on a mission of peace. There can be no question about this. We should not, however, try to make him a pacifist or to label him as a critic of the crusade."[14] Christoph Maier, another leading Crusade scholar, is even more explicit: "Francis thus accepted the Crusade as both legitimate and ordained by God, and he was quite obviously not opposed to the use of violence when it came to the struggle between Christians and Muslims."[15] At one time Francis had remarked to his friars that ". . . paladins and valiant knights who were mighty in battle pursued the infidels even to death . . ." Francis admired the deeds of such brave men because ". . . these holy martyrs died fighting for the Faith of Christ."[16]

As a mark of his great admiration for Francis, or perhaps as a final stratagem, the King next attempted to shower the friar with monetary gifts and attractive presents. In the words of Celano, the Poverello's first biographer, "he tried to bend Francis' mind toward the riches of the world."[17] But the Saint's only interest was the salvation of souls, and he viewed material things with scorn. The Sultan, perhaps seeking to benefit his own soul, pleaded with Francis at least to take these gifts and donate them to poor Christians and to churches. Once again the friar demurred, determined to have nothing whatever to do with money or property.[18] Francis' refusal to accept these presents only served to increase the Sultan's admiration for this bold missionary, who was supremely detached from any desire for money or possessions. Al-Kamil was filled with the highest respect for St. Francis, "and he looked upon him as a man different from all others."[19]

Chapter 12

Deathbed Conversion?

AFTER a stay of many days in the Sultan's camp (he may have remained as long as a month),[1] Francis realized that he could make no further progress in evangelizing al-Kamil. The King had by this time made it abundantly clear that he was not willing to risk his own life, or an open rebellion of his people, by openly embracing Christianity. There were increasing murmurs of discontent among the Sultan's *imams* and others in his court, whose loyalty to Islam caused them to object to the very presence of Francis and Illuminato in their midst. On the other hand, the Sultan feared that Francis' preaching might have quite a different effect on some of the rank-and-file soldiers. He certainly did not want any of his men abandoning their posts and defecting to the Christian army.[2]

The polite and even friendly reception that Francis received in the Sultan's tent convinced Francis that his desire for martyrdom would not be fulfilled. Celano remarks that God was saving Francis for a different type of martyrdom—alluding to the agonizing stigmata he would bear in the final years of his life.[3] However, the Saint's preaching had at least succeeded in sowing the good seed among the Muslims—but was it sown on fertile ground? At any rate it would be up to God to give the increase. "I have planted, Apollo watered, but God gave the increase. Therefore, neither he that planteth is any thing, nor he that watereth; but God that giveth the increase." (*1 Corinthians* 3: 6-7).

Jacques de Vitry wrote that al-Kamil, before dismissing the friar, privately asked him to pray that God would "reveal to me the law and the faith that is the more pleasing to Him."[4] Brother Illuminato remarked that the Sultan, after hearing Francis fervently preach the Gospel, "always had the Christian faith imprinted in his heart."[5] Moreover, there is an early account, which will be related shortly, that al-Kamil ultimately converted on his deathbed to the Christian Faith.

Although Francis had not accepted any money or other tokens of worldly wealth from the Sultan, he did return to the Crusader base camp with two gifts from al-Kamil, the first of which has a special significance, especially in today's world. It was a delicately wrought ivory horn used by Muslims to call the faithful to daily prayer and was also used to summon the Saracen forces to battle.[6] The horn was later decorated with silver rings and chains, and was inventoried at the Basilica in Assisi as far back as 1473. One of these rings bears the inscription, "With this . . . Saint Francis gathered the people together to hear him preach."[7] This horn is still in the possession of the Franciscan Order.[8] In 2003 this horn was shown to Tariq Aziz, a Chaldean Catholic who was then the Iraqi deputy prime minister, during a visit he made to the tomb of the Saint in Assisi.[9]

As a second indication of his esteem for Francis, the Sultan presented him with a permit of safe-passage, which allowed the Poverello to travel anywhere in his domains without hindrance and excused him from paying tribute to local overlords. This seal or *signaculum* was the first authorization from the Muslims favoring the Franciscans. It signaled the beginning of their special relationship, which allowed the friars eventually to obtain custody of the Christian shrines of the Holy Land.[10] According to one account, al-Kamil allowed Francis and his companions to travel and

preach throughout his kingdom, and "he gave them a certain little token so that no one who saw it should harm them."[11]
Although there is little documentation of his travels, it is widely held that the Saint did employ the *signaculum* to visit many of the sacred shrines associated with the life of Christ during his stay in the Middle East. As mentioned previously, his journeys to Egypt and the Holy Land had a debilitating effect on the condition of his eyes, caused in part by the excessive heat and bodily fatigue he endured.[12] Francis' eye problems were made worse by his habitual weeping, as he contemplated with sorrow and contrition the sufferings of Christ and the sins of the world.[13] This affliction remained with him for the remainder of his life, and his eyesight continued to deteriorate until in his last years he was almost totally blind.

When Francis and Illuminato finally took their leave of the Muslim camp, the Sultan ordered that they be accompanied by a contingent of Saracen cavalry as a security precaution and honor guard. The amazement and admiration of the Christians was unbounded as they saw Francis and his companion return after their extended absence, escorted by the Sultan's men, as if they had been conquerors.[14] Undoubtedly, by this time the Crusaders had given them up for dead, martyred at the hands of the enemy. After his return, Francis probably remained with the Christian army until their short-lived capture of Damietta in November 1219.[15] He then commenced his journey to Palestine, apparently making use of the *signaculum* for safe passage, until his departure for Italy.

His visit to the Sultan was immortalized in Dante's *Divine Comedy* by these verses of the *Paradiso*:[16]

. . . and when
He had, through thirst of martyrdom, stood up

> In the proud Soldan's [Sultan's] presence, and there
>   preach'd
> Christ and His followers; but found the race
> Unripen'd for conversion: back once more
> He hasted (not to intermit his toil),
> And reap'd Ausonian [Italian] lands.

Although the Crusaders did finally defeat the Sultan at Damietta, the end result of the Fifth Crusade was a victory for al-Kamil and the Muslim forces. A ten-year truce between the archrivals was negotiated. Damietta was returned to the Sultan, and he showed that he was not what is known today as a fundamentalist or extremist, since he "treated his hostages with the respect befitting their rank and arranged for food for the army."[17] He even personally entertained John of Brienne and other Christian leaders. A large part of the credit for this magnanimity must be attributed to the influence on the Sultan of the preaching, as well as of the very presence, of St. Francis. Reportedly, al-Kamil was criticized by his own people for his tolerant attitude towards Christians and was accused of failing to be a "fervent Muslim."[18]

The Little Flowers of St. Francis (also known as the *Fioretti*) is the most widely read collection of stories about the first Franciscans. It is in this work that the charming and moving depiction of al-Kamil's deathbed conversion to Christianity appears. The *Little Flowers* was compiled about a hundred years after the Saint's death. Raphael Brown, the editor of the definitive modern edition, writes in its introduction that the origin of the book stems from "a direct oral tradition transmitted by several of the Saint's closest friends—Leo, Masseo, and Giles." He adds further that this oral tradition "is in the main reliable" and its historical value, with due reservations, has been acknowledged by major Franciscan scholars.[19]

According to the *Little Flowers,* after Francis completed his travels in the Holy Land, he paid a final visit to al-Kamil before returning to Italy. The Saint informed the Sultan that he was taking leave of his domains and prophesied to him that on his deathbed he would be baptized a Christian. Upon hearing that Francis was to depart, al-Kamil confided to him that he did want to convert to Christianity, but was afraid to do so, since it would mean the death not only of himself, but also of Francis and his companions. He added that such premature deaths would be unfortunate since he had much to do to secure his own salvation, and that there was so much good that Francis could still do. "But show me how I can achieve salvation, and I am ready to obey you in everything."[20]

The Saint then revealed to the Sultan what would take place after his own death. Through the working of Divine Providence, two of his friars would be inspired to journey from afar and seek out the Sultan, in order to instruct him in the True Faith and baptize him. That he would be saved in this way, Francis said, was made known to him by the Lord Jesus Christ. Until then, al-Kamil should do all he could to dispose himself to receive in the future this great grace.

The Saracen King agreed, and Francis and the friars who were with him took leave of the Sultan's realm. Not long afterwards, in 1226, the soul of St. Francis departed his infirm and exhausted body, and took its glorious flight heavenward. Then, about a dozen years after his death, he appeared in a vision to two of his brother friars. In this vision he instructed them to seek out Sultan al-Kamil, in order to administer Holy Baptism to him as had been promised. The pair immediately set out to do the Saint's bidding, and journeyed across the sea to al-Kamil's kingdom.

The aged potentate himself was in his final illness at the time. He had instructed his sentinels to watch the ports for the arrival of two men dressed in Franciscan garb and to bring them at once to his presence. In due time, the two friars were spotted by the lookouts and brought to the quarters of the Sultan, who received them with great joy in his heart. He knew now that his salvation was at hand, as Francis had foretold. The friars, after instructing al-Kamil in the Faith, administered the sacrament of Baptism to the dying Sultan, "and his soul was saved through the merits of St. Francis."[21]

One eighteenth-century biographer, whose work at the time was highly regarded, devoted almost two pages to enumerating the reasons why it is likely that the Sultan was converted: "There is nothing in this legend which is not very probable."[22] However, to twenty-first century man, the story might seem a total fiction, because in today's incredulous, materialistic age it reads like a myth or naïve wishful thinking. Although no historical proof exists to verify the Sultan's conversion, by the same token, no one can say with certainty that it never occurred. The fact that this story is charming does not mean, therefore, that it must be a fable!

Substantial evidence of al-Kamil's enlightened views of Christianity and Western civilization is reflected in the historical record. At the conclusion of the Fifth Crusade and the defeat of the Crusader army, he freed thirty thousand Christian prisoners, ordering that ample provisions be given to all those who wished to return to their own lands.[23] A letter to the Sultan, written by one of those who was liberated, thanks him in these words: "Never before has such a similar example of goodness towards enemy prisoners been spoken of."[24] In 1229 al-Kamil negotiated a peace treaty with the Holy Roman Emperor Frederick II, with whom he was on good terms personally. The Emperor was an extremely learned person, and at one time he had sent some unresolved scientific and astronomical problems to al-Kamil. The Sultan's Egyptian mathematician solved them, and al-Kamil returned the answers along with the gift of a book on astronomy to the Emperor.

Among the terms of the peace treaty of 1229 was the restoration of Jerusalem to the Christians, with Muslims being allowed only in the vicinity of the Islamic holy sites of the city. The treaty between the Emperor and the Sultan was in fact viable, and hostilities between Christians and Muslims basically ceased for the duration of the pact. It was during this period of peace that the Franciscans were able to lay the groundwork for their role in Palestine as custodians of the Christian shrines.[25] Al-Kamil died in 1238, shortly before the treaty expired.

Chapter 13

The Rule of 1221

ALTHOUGH the date is not known for certain, the return of Francis to his homeland probably took place in the Spring or Summer of 1220.[1] Some of the Franciscans in Italy, concerned about serious problems in the Order, had dispatched a messenger to the Saint entreating him to return. This envoy was a lay brother known as Stephen the Simple because of his innocence and piety. He informed Francis that many in the Order were tearfully praying for the return of their spiritual father and teacher to Italy, so that he could resume his personal guidance of the flock. Stephen also reported the upsetting news that numerous brothers were straying from the path of perfection originally indicated by Francis and were neglecting the practice of Holy Poverty and other virtues.[2] In addition, the two vicars that Francis had left in charge of the Order had approved certain constitutions and regulations that were at variance with the original 1209 Rule.[3]

The news reaching him via Stephen the Simple was so disconcerting that Francis decided to end his stay in the Holy Land at once. On his return to Italy, he took with him Brother Elias, Caesar of Speyer, Peter of Catania and a few others.[4] However, not all of the friars returned; some were left behind in the Middle East to buttress the foundation of the Franciscan presence there. In addition to the headquarters of the Syrian Province at St. John of Acre, this included a church and house in the city of Damietta, which had been

assigned to the Franciscans in 1220, during the brief period
that the Crusaders were in possession of the city.[5]

The original Rule of 1209 had been established in the
early years of Francis' calling to be a follower of Christ. Since
the number of those who were attracted to his way of spirituality was increasing dramatically, he had realized that
some formal rule of life and conduct for the growing Order
was necessary. Consequently, he had drawn up a short
decree based on the precepts, counsels and teachings of
Jesus, including many passages from Scripture. Then,
accompanied by some of his companions, he had journeyed to
Rome to seek the Holy Father's approval for the Rule. This
was the occasion of the famous dream of Pope Innocent III,
in which Francis was seen holding up St. John Lateran
Church, the titular church of the Bishop of Rome, in order to
keep it from collapsing. The Holy Father subsequently gave
his verbal approval to the statutes, which consisted essentially of the observance of the Gospel in religious life.
Although this Rule was the guideline for Franciscan life for
a dozen years, there are no known copies of it in existence.[6]

Upon his return from the Holy Land, Francis realized it
was time to update the Rule of 1209, in order to incorporate
the many decisions, resolutions, and proposals that had been
made since its inception. Thus he composed an eloquent revision of the original statutes, which he completed in 1221. He
assigned Brother Caesar of Speyer the task of polishing it
with quotes from Scripture, and the final result is known as
the Rule of 1221. Since it was considered to be an embellish-
ment of the approved Rule of 1209, and because its terminology lacked formality, it was not presented to the Pope for
his consideration.[7] Hence it is commonly known as the *Regula non Bullata*, since it was a rule, *regula,* that was never
officially endorsed by a Papal Bull.

The importance of Chapter XVI of the *Regula non Bul-*

lata, regarding relations with Islam, should not be underestimated. It is the first documented instance of a Catholic religious order specifically calling for a missionary outreach to unbelievers. "It is the first of its kind in the legislation of religious Orders in the Church."[8] Since the original Rule of 1209 has not survived, it cannot be known for certain whether or not that Rule mentioned Muslims or unbelievers. However, it is likely that Chapter XVI in the *Regula non Bullata* was in fact a new addition to the primitive Rule of 1209, based on Francis' personal experience with Islam during his long sojourn in the Middle East.[9] The full text of Chapter XVI is presented at the close of the following summary and commentary.

Chapter XVI is entitled, "On Traveling among Saracens and Other Infidels." It opens with a familiar verse from the Gospel of Matthew, which succinctly describes what the brothers can expect: "Behold I send you as sheep in the midst of wolves. Be ye therefore wise as serpents and simple as doves." (*Matthew* 10:16). In choosing a quotation that speaks of "wolves," Francis is sending a clear warning that the mission to the Saracens is fraught with very real danger. The implication of the passage is clear: for their own safety the friars should avoid giving unnecessary offense to their Muslim hosts by being extremely alert and careful in what they say and do.

In order to emphasize the seriousness of such an undertaking, an injunction immediately follows the opening warning from Scripture. It states that any friar wishing to undertake a mission among unbelievers must obtain the approval of his minister (superior) in the Order. If the minister perceives that the friar is "suitable to be sent," he should grant his permission, aware that he must render an account to the Lord for his decision. The chapter then proposes two possible ways that Franciscans may conduct themselves in Muslim lands in order to fulfill their mission. The first manner of conduct in regard to the Muslims is simply to lead a life of Christian witness, without openly preaching Christ, so "that they cause no arguments or strife." In essence, they would proclaim the Gospel not with words, but by their lives and actions—passively as it were.

The second manner of conducting themselves is a decidedly more positive and active proclamation of the Gospel. The brothers are to proclaim the word of God openly, so that the unbelievers may hear the good news of Jesus Christ as their Redeemer and Saviour, "that they may be baptized and become Christians." Francis implicitly enjoins prudence, since the Rule never states that the Islamic religion itself is to be denounced or criticized. The traditional Church teaching on the necessity of receiving the sacrament of Baptism in order to be saved is underscored at the close of the second paragraph of the chapter by quoting *John* 3:5, "Unless a man be born again of water and the Holy Ghost, he cannot enter into the kingdom of God." Here it is clear that St. Francis intends that the Muslims convert and be baptized.

Gospel verses are then presented to show that the brothers must not be ashamed of Jesus Christ, but rather must confess Him before men. Francis understands the great risk the friars would be taking by openly professing Christ to the Muslims. Yet he indicates that this second manner of conduct is the higher calling, and even a duty: "On behalf of His love they ought to confront their enemies both visible and invisible." Fully aware that martyrdom may await the brothers who openly preach the Good News while in the Middle East, he reminds them that they "have given themselves and surrendered their bodies to the Lord Jesus Christ."

The first manner of conducting themselves among the unbelievers, which enjoins that the friars are to be essentially docile guests in a foreign land, is contained in only one sentence: "One manner is, that they cause no arguments or strife, but be subject 'to every human creature for God's sake' (*1 Peter* 2:13), and confess themselves to be Christians." It is probable that this manner was prescribed as an optional way of conduct for those brothers who were neither called to nor ready for the sacrifice of martyrdom. This way of behavior, seeking to avoid strife and to be peacefully subject to all, is better understood in the light of the Islamic concept of *dhimma.*

In the *Koran,* Christians and Jews are described as "people of the Book," since they have received revelations from God. In Francis' time (as in other eras), the "people of the Book" were allowed by Islamic law to reside and practice their religion in Muslim countries, but were considered second-class persons, known as *dhimmis.* They were generally made to endure humiliating conditions. *Dhimmis* were forced to submit to regulations that included the type of clothing they were allowed to wear, the size of their homes, and the obligatory sheltering of Muslim travelers and soldiers. They were prevented from exhibiting any public displays of their religion other than their identifying garb. Basically, *dhimmis* were forced to live in subjection to Muslims, and risked the death penalty should they proselytize them. Christians were allowed to keep their churches, but could not repair them or erect new ones. In most cases, as subject peoples, the *dhimmis* were forced to pay a tribute, known as a "poll tax" [*sic*] or *jizya,* to the Muslim authorities. Essentially, the choices for the "people of the Book" living in the Middle East were three: convert to Islam, live as *dhimmis,* or face death. The actual application of *dhimma* and *jizya* varied significantly in different historical eras, depending on the countries and their rulers. Some aspects of Islamic law relating to *dhimmitude* remain active today.[10, 11, 12, 13]

It is almost certain that Francis learned this facet of

Islamic law during his journeys in the Middle East and that his first manner of conduct among the Saracens was an accommodation to *dhimma*. Thus, the brothers who chose this manner of conducting themselves spiritually were to accept their status as *dhimmis*, to "cause no arguments or strife," and to refrain from preaching Christ to the Muslims but to confess themselves to be Christians.

While there is essentially only one line in Chapter XVI of the *Regula non Bullata* dealing with the first manner of conduct, the remainder of the chapter is devoted almost exclusively to the second way. As noted above, this manner consists in proclaiming the Gospel explicitly, after it is clear that God is calling them to do so: "when they have seen that it pleases God." The stated goals of this preaching are *first*, to bring those who are far from the Christian Faith to the knowledge of the Omnipotent Creator, the Triune God— Father, Son and Holy Spirit; *second*, that they will come to believe in Jesus Christ as the Redeemer, Saviour, and Son of God; and *finally*, that the unbelievers become baptized Christians, "reborn of water and the Holy Spirit." Evidently Francis was aware that the Muslim concept of God, although monotheistic, does not recognize a Trinity of Divine Persons, nor does it acknowledge the Divinity of Jesus Christ. In the words of Hilaire Belloc, "Mohammed . . . advanced a clear affirmation, full and complete, against the whole doctrine of an incarnate God. . . He eliminated the Trinity altogether."[14]

Two Scripture verses are put forth to show that the friars' actions, or lack thereof, will have eternal consequences. The first encourages the friars to confess Jesus Christ before men, because He said that, in return, "I will also confess him before my Father, who is in Heaven." (*Matthew* 10:32). The second warns against being ashamed of Jesus Christ and His Gospel, because "of him the Son of man shall be ashamed." (*Luke* 9:26).

Chapter XVI certainly does not presuppose that the Franciscans are going to encounter a peace-loving people, open to considering viewpoints about God and religion other than their own. On the contrary, the remainder of the chapter on the mission to the Saracens is replete with biblical quotes designed to dispose the brothers to endure persecutions, including even death. This part of the Rule aptly reflects Francis' own experiences, since he himself had welcomed the palm of martyrdom by embarking on three journeys in order to convert Muslims to Christianity by his preaching. The following Scripture citations as directly quoted below from the Rule specifically deal with laying down one's life for the sake of the Gospel. The first is, "He who will have lost his life for My sake, shall save it for eternal life." (Cf. *Luke* 9:24; *Matthew* 25:46). Second, "and do not fear those who kill the body" (*Matthew* 10:28), "and after that have no more that they can do." (*Luke* 12:4). Thus it is very clear that Francis is completely aware of the potentially grim consequences of preaching Christ to the Muslims.

That the approach of openly proclaiming the Gospel to unbelievers is essentially confrontational is made explicit in another quote that was cited above: "They ought to confront their enemies both visible and invisible." Rather than retreating from this stand by proposing a mission of accommodation and dialogue, St. Francis presents Scriptures that will sustain the brothers in the face of death as they bring the word of God to the unbelievers. That same word of God will fortify them in order that they will not back down from their Gospel mission.

The remaining Scriptural quotations from Chapter XVI are meant to encourage perseverance in the face of adversity. Included is the beatitude from the Sermon on the Mount which calls those blessed who are persecuted for justice' sake. (*Matthew* 5:11). The brothers are reminded that as the

Master was persecuted, so too shall they be (*John* 15:20), and if they are ill-treated in one city, they should flee to another. (*Matthew* 10:23). When these things begin to occur, they should "Rejoice on that day and exult" (*Luke* 6:23), "since your reward is great in heaven." Finally they are encouraged to face these trials with undisturbed patience and are reminded that he who has "persevered until the end, he shall be saved." (*Matthew* 10:22).

Since the terminology of the *Regula non Bullata* of 1221 was not considered canonically accurate and precise, two years later a formal revision of it was drafted. As a consequence, Chapter XVI, "On Traveling among Saracens and Other Infidels," was greatly shortened (and renumbered) in the revision—the Papally approved *Regula Bullata* of 1223. In fact, the relevant section was compressed into just two sentences:

> Let whoever of the friars who, by divine inspiration, wants to go among the Saracens and other infidels, seek permission for that reason from their Ministers provincial. Indeed let the ministers grant permission to go to none, except those whom they see to be fit to be sent.[15]

Fortunately, the detailed description of this important aspect of the Franciscan charism has been preserved in the earlier Rule, the *Regula non Bullata* of 1221. It provides rich insight into the mind and intentions of St. Francis regarding the mission of the brothers to the followers of Islam. It is quite possible that the removal, in the *Regula Bullata* of 1223, of the positive precept of openly proselytizing the Muslims was the result of a more sober and somber assessment by Francis and his Order of this approach. As will be seen in the next chapter, Franciscan missionaries were martyred

even during the lifetime of the Saint. Although estimates
vary, the total number of Franciscans who have since sacri-
ficed their lives during periods of strife in the Holy Land is in
the thousands, of whom about five hundred have been martyred for the Faith.[16, 17]

From the Rule (*Regula non Bullata*) of 1221[18]

Chapter XVI
On Traveling among Saracens and Other Infidels

The Lord says: "Behold I send you as sheep in the midst of
wolves. Therefore, be wise as serpents and simple as doves."
(cf. *Matthew* 10:16). Whence let whatever friar wants to go
among the Saracens and other infidels, go in accord with the
permission of his minister and servant. And let the minister
give them permission and not forbid them, if he has seen
that they are suitable to be sent; for he will be bound to render an account to the Lord (cf. *Luke* 16:2), if in this or in
other things he will have proceed(ed) indiscreetly. Indeed,
the friars who go can conduct themselves spiritually among
them in two manners. One manner is, that they cause no
arguments or strife, but be subject "to every human creature
for God's sake" (*1 Peter* 2:13) and confess themselves to be
Christians. The other manner is that, when they have seen
that it pleases God, they announce the word of God, so that
they may believe in God the Omnipotent, Father and Son
and Holy Spirit, the Creator of all things, (and) in the
Redeemer and Saviour, the Son, and that they may be baptized and become Christians, because "unless a man be born
again of water and the Holy Ghost, he cannot enter the Kingdom of God." (cf. *John* 3:5). These things and others, which
have pleased the Lord, they can say to them and to others,
because the Lord says in the Gospel: "Every man, who con-

fesses Me before men, him I will confess also before My
Father, who is in Heaven." (*Matthew* 10:32). And: "He who is
ashamed of Me and My discourses, of him the Son of man
will also be ashamed, when He will have come in His
Father's majesty and (that) of the Angels." (cf. *Luke* 9:26).
And let all the friars, wherever they are, remember, that
they have given themselves and surrendered their bodies to
the Lord Jesus Christ. And on behalf of His love (*amor*) they
ought to confront their enemies both visible and invisible,
because the Lord says: "He who will have lost his life for My
sake, shall save it (cf. *Luke* 9:24) for eternal life." (*Matthew*
25:46). "Blessed are those who suffer persecution for justice'
sake, for theirs is the Kingdom of Heaven." (*Matthew* 5:10).
"If they have persecuted Me, they will persecute you also."
(*John* 15:20). And: If they persecute you "in one city, flee to
another." (cf. *Matthew* 10:23). "Blessed are you" (*Matthew*
5:11), "when men have hated you" (*Luke* 6:22) "and cursed
you" and do persecute you (cf. *Matthew* 5:11) "and have separated you and reproached you and cast your name out as
evil" (*Luke* 6:22), "and when they have said every evil
against you, untruly for My sake." (*Matthew* 5:11). "Rejoice
on that day and exult" (*Luke* 6:23), "since your reward is
great in heaven" (cf. *Luke* 12:4), and I "say to you My friends,
do not be afraid of them" (cf. *Luke* 12:4), "and do not fear
those who kill the body" (*Matthew* 10:28) "and after that
have nothing more to do." (*Luke* 12:4). "See, that you are not
disturbed." (*Matthew* 24:6). For "in your patience you shall
possess your souls" (*Luke* 21:19), and the one who "will have
persevered until the end, he shall be saved." (*Matthew* 10:22;
24:13).

Chapter 14

The First Franciscan Martyrs

THE second mode of conduct described in Chapter XVI of the *Regula non Bullata* or Rule of 1221 is that the Gospel should be proclaimed fearlessly. However, the Rule does not propose that the brothers should refute specific Islamic beliefs or engage in controversies, disputes or arguments. Nor is there any suggestion that they are to prepare themselves for this mission by studying the *Koran* or other sources of Islamic doctrine. They are enjoined simply to preach what they know and believe, the good news of Jesus Christ as God and Saviour, in order that the Saracens become baptized Christians. In its wonderful Franciscan simplicity this is a wholly positive response to Christ's command to bring the Gospel to all creatures: "Going therefore, teach ye all nations; baptizing them in the name of the Father, and of the Son, and of the Holy Ghost. Teaching them to observe all things whatsoever I have commanded you. . ." (*Matthew* 28:19-20).

This very practical and cautious outlook may have had its origin in certain violent incidents that had already occurred prior to the formulation of the Rule of 1221, when the earliest Franciscan missioners had openly derided the Islamic beliefs. Francis' contemporary, Jacques de Vitry, wrote his esteemed *History of the Orient* at about this time. In it he mentions that the Muslims were receptive to the Franciscans who preached about Christ and explained the teachings of the Gospel. However, when "their preaching attacked

Mohammed and openly condemned him as a liar and a traitor, then these ungodly men heaped blows upon them and chased them from their cities." Vitry wrote that the Franciscans would have been killed if God had not intervened to miraculously protect them.[1]

In 1218, a year before Francis left on his journey to Damietta, two of the brothers, Egidio and Eletto, were sent to preach Christ to the Saracens in Tunisia, North Africa.[2] Eletto was especially eager for this mission since he had heard that "The Saracens treated with great cruelty those Christians who spoke ill of the law of Mahomet."[3] After arriving in Tunisia, the two brothers publicly proclaimed the Faith for some time, until Muslim reactionaries began to call for the death of these men who dared to speak against their prophet. Although the Franciscans were prepared to suffer martyrdom, the Christian community that had been housing them feared that they, too, would be included in the impending bloodshed. Consequently, they forcibly took the friars on board a vessel that was to set sail for Italy, and would not let them off until the boat departed. However, Eletto, either escaping the ship or returning to Africa later, continued to preach to the Muslims on that continent. After some years, he obtained his longed-for palm of glory, by the sword of a Saracen. Before being struck, he humbly knelt while holding onto the Franciscan Rule and confessed his guilt and sorrow for any transgressions against it.[4]

Eletto's martyrdom is believed to have occurred many years after the Franciscan Rules of 1221 and 1223 were established, and perhaps even after the death of St. Francis. Thus, his fate had no effect on the contents of either Rule. However, the dramatic martyrdom of five Franciscans in Morocco in 1220 must have had a significant impact on the wording of Chapter XVI of the *Regula non Bullata* a year later. It may have also been responsible for the subsequent downplay of the mission to the

Muslims in the revised Rule of 1223.

It was at the General Chapter of the friars in 1219 that Francis assigned to himself the task of preaching to the Muslims in the East, and shortly afterwards he began his journey to Damietta. At that same General Chapter, half a dozen men from the Order were chosen to witness to the Saracens toward the West, having as their goal the North African country of Morocco. Appointed to be in charge of this group was a pious brother by the name of Votalis; his five companions were the Saints Berard, Peter, Accursius, Adjutus and Otho. Berard is said to have known some Arabic, and Peter and Otho may have been priests.[5] Prior to their departure on this mission, Francis spoke to them at length. He prefaced his discourse with the following words: "My dear children, it is God who has commanded me to send you amongst the Saracens, to make known His faith, and refute the law of Mahomet. I shall go in a different direction to work for the conversion of the same infidels, and thus I shall send preachers over the whole earth."[6] After giving many counsels and exhortations, he closed by entreating them to keep in mind the Passion of Christ, which would strengthen them in the sufferings ahead.[7, 8]

The six friars then set out for Spain. However, when they reached the Kingdom of Aragon in the north-central part of the country, Votalis became seriously ill, and was forced to abandon the mission. The remaining five proceeded toward the southwest, into territory occupied by the Muslims, or Moors, as the Spanish called them. With their religious habits concealed beneath secular clothes, the friars entered the town of Seville, where they remained hidden for a week at the home of a Christian.[9]

Finally, their caution overcome by their zeal, they burst forth from the house and attempted to enter the principal mosque of Seville. There, their preaching was met with beatings, and they were forced back. Undeterred, they sought an audience with the Muslim emir, who tolerated their attempts to have him convert and be baptized, until the five friars began openly to deride Mohammed. They were briefly confined to the top of a tower, but after loudly proclaiming Jesus to those entering the palace below, they were moved to the ground floor and later brought before the sheik. They were offered complete pardon if they would renounce Christianity in favor of Islam, but answered that they preferred death. Seeing their stubbornness, the sheik and his court decided to banish them to Morocco, which ironically was their original destination.

There, they encountered Don Pedro, the self-exiled brother of the King of Portugal. This Christian prince, who was in the service of the Muslim king of Morocco, Miramolino, received them with respect—but tried without success to dissuade them from preaching Christ to the people. Berard, in particular, stood upon a wagon and began railing against Islam, and he continued doing so even as Miramolino and his cortege were passing by. Thinking that the friar must be mad, the king ordered all five of the brothers out of the country. But the Franciscans escaped on their way to the port. When they resumed their preaching, they were imprisoned at Marrakech by the Muslim ruler.[10]

After twenty days of confinement, where they were deprived of all food and water, they were finally released. To the astonishment of their captors, they " . . . came out in full health and strength."[11] After a long series of imprisonments, escapes, and more preaching, accompanied by reports of miracles, the king had the five friars bound and brought into his presence. He offered them large sums of money and beautiful women if they would only embrace the Islamic religion. Otho is reported to have replied, "Mohammed guides you on a false and lying path, to the place of eternal death where he is tormented along with his followers."[12] After listening to this and to protestations of their willingness to die for the Christian Faith, the king despaired of ever converting them to Islam. With his own hands he angrily grabbed his scimitar and cleaved the heads of all five Franciscans. It was January 16, 1220, a date now memorialized in the Church as the feast of the Moroccan Martyrs, Saints Berard and his Companions. They were canonized in 1481 by Pope Sixtus IV, their sanctity confirmed by many miracles.[13]

The remains of the martyrs were taken to Portugal, where they were placed amid great ceremony in the Augustinian monastery of the Regular Canons of the Holy Cross (Santa Cruz), at Coimbra. Residing at that time in the monastery was a diligent student of the Scriptures named Fernando Bouillon of Lisbon. Inspired by the presence of the relics and the story of the bravery of the Franciscans, he left the cloister of the Canons and joined the Order of Friars Minor. He took the name of Anthony, and attempted to follow in the footsteps of the five martyrs by preaching in Morocco. He reached Marrakech but was forced to abandon his plans due to a serious illness. The ship that was to carry him back to Portugal was driven off course by a storm, and he landed on the shores of Italy. Making his way to Assisi, the future St. Anthony of Padua was eventually permitted by Francis to teach theology to the brethren because of his great learning and his brilliance as a preacher.[14, 15]

When the news reached Francis of the deaths of the five Moroccan martyrs, his reaction was: "Now I can truly say I have five brothers."[16] However, he did not wish his followers to dwell on the deeds and martyrdom of their confreres as a substitute for fulfilling their own Christian mission. On one occasion, when the story of the five martyrs was brought before him, he did not want it to be read, saying, "Each one should glory in his own suffering and not in someone else's."[17] The importance of pursuing Christian virtue not only in word, but also in deed, was a recurring theme for St. Francis. He was truly committed to living out his faith, and did not want his brothers doing so vicariously. Yet, he desired them to be prudent in preaching the Word. One thirteenth-century writer speculated that Francis did not want to hear the story of the Moroccan martyrs because he was shocked at the way they had insulted Islam. Specifically, after Otho accused Mohammed of leading his followers to the place of eternal torment, the friar then spit on the ground while invoking the name of the Prophet.[18] Francis was aware that explicit condemnations of the Muslim religion could only result in closing the minds and hearts of his hearers to the good news of Christianity. However, it is clear from statements attributed to him that the reason he did not want to dwell on the martyrdom of the Moroccan martyrs was his preference for action over words. In fact, commenting on the Saints of the Church in one of his own writings, the *Admonitions*, he lamented that "We who are servants of God try to win honor and glory by recounting and making known what they have done."[19]

As mentioned earlier, Francis had at one time observed that "paladins and valiant knights who were mighty in battle pursued the infidels even to death." Francis admired such brave men because "These holy martyrs died fighting for the Faith of Christ." He added: "We see many today who would like to attribute honor and glory to themselves by being content with singing about the exploits of others."[20] Although the present book is not a study of the different interpretations that have been put forth over the centuries* about

---

* A book in French by University of Nantes Professor John V. Tolan discusses the different interpretations of Francis' historic visit to the Sultan. It examines the works of writers and artists over the past eight centuries. An English translation is expected in 2008, according to the

Francis' visit to the Sultan, it is interesting to note what a contemporary theologian has to say about the preceding quotes. The revisionist Franciscan scholar J. Hoeberichts states that these comments sound "very strange, if not entirely impossible, in the mouth of Francis."[21] What really *is* "strange" is that eight hundred years after the fact, someone would dispute the recollections of the author of the anecdote, Brother Leo, who was alive at the time and was one of Francis' closest friends![22] Apparently, today's "politically correct" St. Francis could not possibly have praised men who died in battle in defense of Christianity.

In contrast to Hoebericht's view is the eyewitness testimony of Jacques de Vitry, who was with the Franciscans during the battle of Damietta. He observed: "They do not withhold their sword from blood: they fight, they travel through the city in all directions." He also wrote: "These are the men whom, in our opinion, the Lord has raised up in these latter times to battle against the Antichrist . . . for day and night, without interruption, they devote themselves to praising God or to preaching." They "raise their voice like a trumpet."[23] But for the revisionists, the "real" Francis was not a bold Christian evangelist, but a timid man, whose goal was to have the friars live passively among the Saracens and "to be subject to them," rather than convert them to the True Religion.[24]

Francis himself, in the above cited *Admonitions*, praises the Saints who followed Christ "in trials and persecutions, in ignominy, hunger and thirst, in humiliations and temptations, and so on."[25] These are not the words of someone who would forgo the salvation of unbelievers in favor of dialogue and appeasement, as part of a policy of mutual

author. *Saint Francis et le Sultan: Une rencontre vue à travers huit siècles de textes et images* (Paris: Seuil, 2007)—*St. Francis and the Sultan: A Meeting Viewed over Eight Centuries of Writings and Images.*

accommodation. St. Francis' dialogue with the Sultan was a dialogue of conversion to Jesus Christ, not a dialogue of finding common ground in order for the two religions to co-exist peacefully. As noted previously, the passive aspect of the ministry to the Saracens applied only to those brothers who were neither called nor ready to face possible martyr-dom by preaching to them. But for Francis himself, the mis-sion to unbelievers had only one goal—their conversion to Christianity. This was the desired fruit. According to one of the early sources, St. Francis frequently repeated the say-ing: "A man's knowledge is revealed by his actions, and the words of a Religious must be supported by his own deeds, for the test of the tree is in its fruit."[26]

PART THREE
The Stigmatist

"Besides all this, no matter whether he was well or ill, he treated his body with the greatest severity; he used to call his body "my brother the ass"; nor could he be induced to give himself any relief or rest, not even when, as during the last years of his life, he was suffering greatly, the sufferings of one nailed to a cross, for he had become like unto Christ because of the stigmata which he bore."
—Pope Pius XI, *Rite Expiatis*, no 27.*

---

* http://www.vatican.va/holy_father/pius–xi/encyclicals/documents/hf_p-xi_enc_30041926_rite-expiatis_en.html.

Chapter 15

The Crèche of Greccio

BEFORE describing the last years of Francis' life, which were crowned with the gift of the stigmata, let us note some incidents deserving of mention which occurred after he returned from his final trip to the Middle East.

Upon re-entering Italy in 1220, one of the first places Francis visited was the city of Bologna. The University of Bologna at that time was the center of learning for all of Europe, with an enrollment of 10,000 students.[1] Francis wished to visit the place of his friars located near the gates of the city, but was extremely disturbed when told that it was called "The House of the Friars," as if it were a stately edifice under their ownership. Upon seeing it, he refused even to stay in the town and spent the night with the Dominicans.[2] He was displeased because the house was too imposing a place for those who were espoused to Holy Poverty. To make matters worse, one of the friars, Giovanni da Sciacca, who in the world had been a doctor of law, was trying to establish the Franciscans' residence as a house of studies. This was anathema to Francis, who did not wish his Order to be focused on the reading of books and scholarly pursuits, but rather on prayer and simple living. He firmly rebuked friar Giovanni in these words: "You want to destroy my Order! I have always desired and willed, after the example of my Lord Jesus Christ, that my brothers would prefer to pray rather than to read."[3]

He ordered all of the brothers to vacate that building

immediately, including many ill friars who were being tended there. Among the infirm was one of the first followers of the Poverello, Brother Leo, who wrote an account of the incident. They hastened to obey, and it was only when the Papal Legate, Cardinal Ugolino, intervened and placated Francis that the friars were able to return. The Cardinal explained that the large airy rooms helped restore health to the sick, and he assured the Saint that the property did not belong to the friars. In fact, he declared that he would secure the ownership of the place in the name of the Church. This appeased the Saint, and he allowed the brothers to return to the house, but he refused to enter it himself.[4, 5]

Once when asked if some of the more educated brothers who had joined the Order should continue their studies of Sacred Scripture, St. Francis' answer was: "I do not mind, provided that they do not neglect prayer, after the example of Christ, of whom we are told He prayed more than He studied."[6] Francis himself never had formal instruction in theology or biblical studies, but he often read the Scriptures and meditated on their meaning. His exceptional memory and keen intellect, combined with the enlightenment and grace bestowed from above, gave him a profound understanding of the sacred mysteries. A doctor of theology consulted him at one time in Siena about some difficult questions, and the answers that Francis expounded were so amazing that this learned scholar exclaimed, "His theology soars aloft on the wings of purity and contemplation, like an eagle in full flight."[7]

The Poverello resigned as Superior of the Friars Minor in 1220, possibly at the time of the General Chapter held that September. This freed him from administrative responsibilities, although he still remained the spiritual head of the Order. He appointed Brother Peter of Catania as Minister General. Francis demonstrated his great humility by reverently bowing down before the new Superior, vowing his obedience. Many of the friars who were present wept in dismay at this unexpected turn of events, but the Saint reassured them by commending the Order to the care of God and to the ministers. According to the primary sources, the reasons for his resignation were his bodily infirmities and his desire to remain the humblest and least of the brothers. Another likely factor, however, was the increased time and attention required for overseeing the ever-expanding Order, which detracted from his efforts at preaching and prayer.[8]

The Order had undergone phenomenal growth since the first dozen or so friars had made the journey to Rome in 1209, to seek approval for the original Rule of the fledgling community. In fact, at the General Chapter of 1221, known as the Chapter of Mats, more than five thousand friars were in attendance.[9] Unfortunately, this rapid growth was accompanied by a relaxation in discipline. Many of the brothers were beginning to drift spiritually in diverse directions, not always following the Gospel commitment to poverty and simplicity. For example, some of them sought to live according to a regulated monastic fashion, while others wanted theological studies to be emphasized. Francis saw the need for a new and expanded Rule, which would provide clearer direction for the friars and would reflect his wishes for the way the Order should be guided and develop. It was under these circumstances that the *Regula non Bullata*, the Rule of 1221, came about. This was further revised in 1223, and was confirmed by Honorius III in the Papal Bull *"Solet Annuere,"* on November 29 of that year.

The Rule of 1223—the *Regula Bullata*—still technically remains in effect almost eight centuries later! Although today's Franciscan communities observe mitigated versions of it, this ancient Rule of the Friars Minor endures as a living testimony to the genius of its founder. Francis himself received a special call to give precedence to the active life; however, for a brother who is following the Rule, the "form of life is primarily and essentially contemplative and includes the obligation of a life of prayer and fasting." Further, "the life is constituted by personal and communal poverty, and the observance of that which Pope St. Innocent XI called 'the chief precept' of the Rule of St. Francis: the non-use of money."[10]

Less than a month after the papal approval of the *Regula Bullata*, Francis arrived at the brothers' hermitage in the little town of Greccio—a community in the vicinity of Rieti, located about halfway between Assisi and Rome. It was now December, and Francis had long been nurturing a heartfelt desire to celebrate Christmas in a wonderful new manner. He wanted others to share his own inner joy and exaltation at what for him was the most important feast of the year, since our salvation was heralded by the birth of Christ. He conceived of a simple way to awaken everyone's love and admiration of the Christ Child, especially those who were weak in the Faith.[11]

His plan was to have Christmas Midnight Mass celebrated in the presence of a realistic representation of the humble grotto of Bethlehem, complete with live animals. "For I wish to do something that will recall to memory the little Child who was born in Bethlehem and set before our bodily eyes in some way the inconveniences of his infant needs."[12] According to St. Bonaventure, he even obtained the approval of Pope Honorius, so that he would not be accused of willfully introducing novelty into the sacred ceremonies.[13]

Francis had arranged beforehand to have his friend, the nobleman Giovanni Velita, make the necessary preparations and help spread word of the event.[14] A little manger or crib was set up in the woods near the hermitage, filled with the common, coarse hay that beasts of burden feed upon. An ox and an ass were then led to the place. Some later embellishments of the story maintain that figures of Mary and Joseph were also positioned about the manger.[15] Francis was delighted to see everything ordered as he had wished. To the Poverello, "The sight of the crèche [manger scene] in its glorious simplicity was a symbol of the advent of lowliness, the exaltation of poverty, the praise of humility."[16]

A host of brothers from near and afar descended upon Greccio, arriving from numerous friaries and villages. They joined with the crowds of local residents, field workers, and shepherds; all were drawn toward the manger where Francis knelt. The candles and torches of the onlookers brightened up the crisp night, reflecting their glow upon a light snow that had begun to fall. The sound of hymns echoed in the hollows and woodlands. Men and beasts and even nature itself radiated great joy on that special Christmas Eve—it was truly the feast of hearts. "The woods rang with the voices of the crowd and the rocks made answer to their jubilation."[17]

The Holy Sacrifice of the Mass was celebrated at midnight with great solemnity, using an altar that had been erected over the manger. Francis, vested in his Deacon's robes, sang the Gospel in a voice characterized by Celano as sweet, clear, strong and sonorous.[18]

He preached a touching sermon, describing the first Christmas and the humble surroundings of Mary and Joseph at the nativity of the Son of God, whom he lovingly referred to as the Child of Bethlehem. During the ceremony, Giovanni Vileta experienced a vision in which he saw a babe lying in the crib, rapt in a slumber so deep that he appeared lifeless. Then he saw St. Francis approach and take the child in his arms, rousing him from his sleep.[19] For his biographer Celano, this vision aptly symbolized the mission of the Saint:

"for the Child Jesus had been forgotten in the hearts of many; but, by the working of His grace, He was brought to life again through His servant St. Francis and stamped upon their fervent memory."[20]

The after-glow from that evening of devotion was manifested throughout the area in the days that followed. Many miraculous healings occurred among the sick, who were prayed over and touched with some of the hay that had lain in the sacred manger. Even infirm animals that were given the stalks of that hallowed grass for their food were restored to health. The influence and "after-glow" of that night in 1223 persists to this day, since it is generally accepted that the popular custom of Christmas Eve crèches—mangers, nativity cribs—was inaugurated by St. Francis in Greccio.

Chapter 16

Seal of the Living God

"AND I saw another angel, ascending from the rising of the sun, having the sign of the living God; and he cried with a loud voice to the four angels, to whom it was given to hurt the earth and the sea, saying: Hurt not the earth, nor the sea, nor the trees, till we sign the servants of our God in their foreheads." (*Apocalypse* 7:2-3.)

The great Doctor of the Church, St. Bonaventure, applied this Scripture prophecy to St. Francis, who would bear on his body the sign and seal of the Crucified God. "Therefore, there is every reason to believe that it is he who is referred to under the image of an Angel coming up from the east, with the seal of the living God, in the prophecy made by another friend of Christ the Bridegroom, St. John the Apostle and Evangelist."[1] In his *Paradiso*, Dante speaks of Assisi as the East, a word-play on *Ascesi,* an ancient name of Assisi, meaning "I have risen."[2]

> . . . therefore let none, who speak
> Of that place, say Ascesi; for its name
> Were lamely so deliver'd; but the East,
> To call things rightly, be it henceforth styl'd.

Finally, the Church labels the Poverello the Patron Saint of Ecology and Animals. Thus St. Francis virtually fulfills to the letter the prophecy of this Angel of the Apocalypse, rising from the East, bearing the seal of the Living God and protecting creation from harm.

105

Two years before his death, Francis, with a small group of his closest companions, ascended a remote peak high in the Apennines of Tuscany, about 55 miles from Assisi. The wealthy Count Orlando of Chiusi, in thanksgiving and appreciation for guidance he had received from the Saint, had donated the mountainous crag to Francis for use as a spiritual retreat. It was mid-summer in 1224 when Francis chose to climb this solitary precipice called La Verna (in Latin, *Alverna*), in order to make a forty-day fast in preparation for Michaelmas, the September 29th feast of St. Michael. At that time, this fast was known as the Lent of St. Michael, and it began on August 15, the feast of the Assumption of the Blessed Virgin Mary. Among the trusted companions Francis took with him on this spiritual pilgrimage were Brothers Masseo, Angelo and Leo, and probably a few others, including Brother Illuminato.[3]

St. Francis wished to use this precious time on the isolated mount to come ever closer to the Lord Jesus in prayer and meditation. In order better to "pray without ceasing" and to avoid unnecessary interruptions, he had a solitary little hut built for himself, located at some distance from where his companions would be staying. Brother Leo was the only one allowed to visit Francis' cell, dropping off a little bread and water once a day. He was also to come and join him at the hour for night prayer (Matins). But whenever he approached the lodging of the Saint, Leo was first to call out to him and could come closer only when the Saint signaled his consent. Francis established this arrangement because he was often rapt in ecstasy and in heavenly contemplation and thus not aware of the things of this earth, being unable to speak or hear. When in this state, he did not wish any of the brothers to disturb him or witness his secret colloquies with the Lord. "He shall dwell on high; the fortifications of rocks shall be his highness: Bread is given him, his waters are sure." (*Isaias* 33:16).

In addition to the angelic and divine communications with which the Lord gifted him on this most holy retreat, the demons were also permitted to torment him. One day, while he was engrossed in prayer in a little rocky niche that overlooked a steep drop, a hideous devil appeared before him. This fierce creature from the netherworld began to beat Francis, in an attempt to hurl the body of the Saint onto boulders below. Francis was in grave danger of tumbling over the edge of the cliff. Turning his face to avoid having to look at the frightening specter, he clutched the side of the rock face, in a vain effort to grab onto an outcropping for support. However, there were no protrusions he could cling to, and he began slipping toward the rim. But suddenly, the rock seemed to soften and open up as if to welcome him. His hands, face and body begin to sink into the stone like objects pressed into melted wax. This miraculous transformation of the rock enabled him to grasp the side of the cliff, and in this way he was saved from the demon's assault. The marks of his hands were said to be still visible on the stone almost two hundred years later.[4] "The mountains shall be moved from the foundations with the waters: the rocks shall melt as wax before thy face." (*Judith* 16:18).

During his stay on La Verna, there were also many pleasant encounters—since those famous conversations of Francis with God's creatures were not wanting. When he first arrived there, a flock of various kinds of birds joyfully circled his cell, greeting him in song. This warm welcome caused Francis to remark: "I see that it is God's will we should stay here, our sisters the birds are so glad to see us."[5] The rocky crags were a favorite habitat for falcons, known for swooping down on their prey. One in particular nested near the isolated cell where Francis had chosen to spend his prayerful solitude. The bird began to keep Francis company "in a tame way" during the day, and quickly learned Francis' routine of

rising during the night before dawn for Matins.[6] Soon,
Brother Alarm Clock began to sing and noisily flap his wings
at that hour, continuing the racket until the Saint awoke.
Francis was delighted with this performance, since it drove
away any laziness or reluctance on his part to rise so early.
However, if the friar were ill or weaker than usual, the fal-
con, as if instructed by an Angel of God, would not commence
singing until after sunrise. Celano, noting this wonderful
arrangement, makes this splendid observation: "Little wonder if all other creatures too venerated this eminent lover of
the Creator."[7]

His early biographers report a prophetic incident involving Francis that took place either at Mount La Verna, or just
prior to his sojourn there. As he had often done in the past,
Francis wished to determine God's will for him by opening
up the Scriptures at random, and reading the verses that
appeared before his eyes. "To prove that neither he nor his
disciples were ever to be separated from Our Lord, he always
had recourse to the Gospels as to an oracle whenever he had
to make a decision on any matter." (Pope Pius XI).[8]

On this occasion, after lifting his heart up to God in
prayer, he had the Gospels brought to him by a friar. He (or
possibly his companion) then opened the book "with reverence and fear."[9] The page that his eyes fell on at this first
opening told of the suffering and death of Christ. But Francis wanted confirmation of this disconcerting outcome, so the
book was closed, and the process was repeated a second and
then a third time. Each time the page opened to the story of
the Passion. Francis, who had faithfully followed in the footsteps of the public life and preaching of Jesus, understood
this to mean that he was now to follow the Lord in the ascent
of Mount Calvary.[10] Although he was barely forty years old,
he foresaw that the time of his own suffering and death was
nearing. But it was not yet revealed to him in what manner

he was to be crucified with Christ.

September 14, the Feast of the Exaltation of the Cross, was approaching. On the preceding day, Francis had a vision of an Angel who spoke some disquieting words to him: "I encourage you and urge you to prepare and dispose yourself humbly to receive with all patience what God wills to do in you."[11] The Saint answered that he was prepared to endure all that the Lord wished of him. Apparently satisfied with this reply, the Angel departed. At dawn on the day of the feast, Francis emerged from his cell on the mountain and remained for a long time steeped in prayer. The nature and intention of his meditation that morning was divulged many years later to a Franciscan of "great holiness." This friar was Brother John of Alverna who, after the death of Francis, was graced with an apparition of the Saint.[12] In this vision, Francis revealed to Brother John that he had asked the Lord for two great graces while he was on Mount La Verna—favors that only a person who possessed a truly seraphic love of God would dare ask, or even conceive of asking. The first was that he would feel in his own soul *and his body*, as much as possible, all the pain and suffering that Jesus experienced during His Passion on the Cross. The second grace asked by Francis was that he be allowed to experience in his heart the great love that Jesus had for sinful mankind, a love so excessive that it would lead Him to endure willingly such intense suffering for our Redemption. As he prayed, he was given to understand that God had acceded to his request, and would allow him to experience these two favors as much as possible for "a mere creature."[13]

Francis continued with his solitary prayer and meditation as the morning progressed, contemplating the mystery of Christ's overwhelming love and suffering. Then, as he gazed heavenward, he saw descending rapidly from on high what seemed to be an angelic being all aflame. As it approached

from above, he could see that it bore the six fiery wings of the
Seraphim, the highest of the nine choirs of angels. This mysterious personage grew closer, until it hovered right before
his eyes. Francis could clearly discern that the Seraph was
in the form of a Man, having hands and feet affixed to a
cross. Two of the wings were raised over his head, the two at
his side were extended for flight, and the third pair of wings
extended over much of his body down to his feet.[14]

The Seraphim are described in Scripture as "living creatures" who minister at the very throne of the Most High,
praising God as thrice holy. In *Isaias* it is written of the
Seraphim: "And they cried one to another, and said: Holy,
holy, holy, the Lord God of hosts, all the earth is full of His
glory." (*Isaias* 6:3). The *Apocalypse* reveals that God is
praised for evermore by four living creatures, each with six
wings. "And they rested not day and night, saying: Holy, holy,
holy, Lord God Almighty, who was, and who is, and who is to
come." (*Apocalypse* 4:8). In answer to the question as to why
a Seraph was sent to Francis, since a Seraph was not crucified for us, St. Bonaventure responds: "A Seraph is a spirit
who is so called because of his fervent love, and the fact that
a Seraph was sent to St. Francis means that he was on fire
with the ardor of love."[15]

The Seraph looked at him with benevolence and compassion, which filled the Saint's heart with profound joy. But at
the same time, seeing that the creature was cruelly fastened
to a cross, his joy was mixed with a certain sorrow and
anguish. He was filled with wonder and amazement at the
vision, and could not comprehend what it meant, or how a
seraphic entity from Heaven could be afflicted in such a way.
St Bonaventure declared that the apparition was of Jesus
Himself: "He was overjoyed at the way Christ regarded him
so graciously under the appearance of a Seraph."[16] Finally,
by divine inspiration, Francis understood the significance of

the vision: it meant that he himself would be transformed by his seraphic love for God into a perfect image of Christ Crucified.[17]

In His unfathomable wisdom, the Heavenly Father then wrought in Francis a new and hitherto unheard-of miracle and prodigy. He sent a sign and a confirmation to the Church and to the whole world, to demonstrate how pleased He was with the love of Francis for His crucified Son. God in His great mercy wished to signify that Francis had fulfilled perfectly the Gospel precept taught by Jesus Christ: "And calling the multitude together with his disciples, he said to them: If any man will follow me, let him deny himself, and take up his cross, and follow me." (*Mark* 8:34). Hence, on the hands, feet and side of St. Francis, the Most High imprinted the sacred marks of the crucifixion of Jesus—the stigmata. The Saint's hands and feet were pierced through the middle, and on his right side an open and bloody wound appeared. Francis later disclosed that the Lord had said: "I have given you the emblems of My Passion so that you may be My standard-bearer."[18]

Not only was Francis the first person in the history of the Church to be graced with the five wounds of Christ, but there was a uniqueness about his wounds which has never been duplicated in the many stigmatists that have followed him.[19]* The flesh on the inside of the palm of each hand and on the instep of each foot was formed in the shape of the head of a nail, whereas on the opposite side of his hands and feet, the pointed ends of these mysterious nails rose above his flesh a short distance and then were bent back. "The heads were black and round, but the points were long and

---

* Some interpret the following Scripture verse to mean that St. Paul the Apostle received the stigmata, although there is no corroborating evidence or report: "From henceforth let no man be troublesome to me, for I bear the marks of the Lord Jesus in my body." (*Galatians* 6:17).

bent back, as if they had been struck with a hammer."[20]

The seraphic vision also communicated certain wonderful secrets to the Saint, which Francis refused to reveal to anyone while he was still alive. However, after his death, Francis appeared to a devout friar (not the aforementioned Brother John of Alverna), who had prayed for eight years to learn something of the secrets. Francis disclosed to this friar that, just as Christ descended to the netherworld after His crucifixion to free the souls of the just, and ushered them into Heaven, the Lord had promised Francis a similar bounty. Jesus assured him that by the merits and virtue of the holy stigmata, "Every year on the day of your death you may go to Purgatory and . . . draw out of there all the souls of your three Orders" and lead them to their heavenly reward.[21] Thus the Saint would be conformed in death as well as in life to the Saviour. Francis told the friar that he had kept this a secret while he was still alive so that he would not be accused of boasting and vainglory.[22]

The Poverello knew that it would be virtually impossible to keep the existence of his holy wounds hidden from his companions. The end of the forty-day fast was nigh, and Francis would have to emerge from his solitude and descend the mountain together with his brother friars. However, he feared that any special attention or affection shown him would cause him to lose favor with God, to whom all glory and honor is due: "But, lest human favor should steal any of the grace given him, he strove in every way he could to hide it."[23] Consequently, at first he attempted to hide the stigmata by keeping his hands and feet covered, but the friars quickly noticed his unusual difficulty in walking. Also, it was the custom for the brothers to wash the habit and breeches of Francis, upon which were now visible the bloodstains from his wounds.

Uncertain as to his course of action, he consulted with his

companions. Speaking only in general terms, he asked them whether it was wise to reveal something spiritual that had recently befallen him. Then that same Brother Illuminato— who years before had advised Francis to reveal to the Crusaders his prophecy of the disastrous outcome of a looming battle (Chapter 9)—spoke out. Enlightened by God, Illuminato realized that something wonderful had happened to Francis, something that the whole world should know about. He explained to him that the revelations given him by God were often meant for others, too, and reminded the Saint of the parable of the talents, and the sorry fate of the man who had buried his.[24, 25]

Francis humbly accepted this advice from Illuminato. He took it as a sign from God to reveal to this group of his closest friars the news of the great and unheard-of gift of the stigmata that had been bestowed on him. This he did in conformity with the Scripture which counseled, "For it is good to hide the secret of a king, but honorable to reveal and confess the works of God." (*Tobias* 12:7). On the other hand, although he told those few who were with him on La Verna what had happened, he only permitted one of them ever to see the wounds. This fortunate man was Brother Leo, chosen by the Saint to wrap the lesions with bandages, which were changed often because of the blood they continually absorbed. Since the wrappings provided Francis with some comfort and relief from the pain of the wounds, he would not let Brother Leo change them from Thursday evening until Saturday morning. He wished to embrace fully the pains of Christ's Passion in his own body during that time in which our Saviour was arrested, suffered, died, and was buried.[26] "With Christ I am nailed to the cross. And I live, now not I; but Christ liveth in me." (*Galatians* 2:19-20).

The gift of the sacred wounds was bestowed on Francis on or about September 14, the feast of the Exaltation of the

Cross, also referred to as the Triumph of the Cross. To com-
memorate that great event of the autumn of 1224, the
Church honors the Stigmata of St. Francis on September 17.

Chapter 17

Glorious Transitus

THE remarkable apparition of Christ in the form of a Seraph took place before sunrise, causing Mount La Verna to be all-aglow, as it shone with the glory of God's visitation. Shepherds tending their flocks during the night reported that the mountain seemed to be wrapped in flames for more than an hour. Some muleteers staying at a hostel in the area actually rose from their beds thinking it was dawn. News of the marvelous phenomenon traveled quickly and served to increase the expectation and joy felt throughout the countryside when, two weeks later, word spread that "the Saint" was descending the mountain![1]

Here Francis began his passage into glory, riding on a donkey loaned to him by a peasant, because his wounded feet were unable to support him. The populace lined the paths and byways to catch a glimpse of the now-famous man of God as he passed by. They were drawn from all of the surrounding districts, hoping to experience the sense of wonder, joy and awe that came from simply being in the presence of the Holy Man of Assisi.

They knew nothing of the stigmata as yet—he now wore socks with his sandals, and his pierced hands were bandaged and partly concealed by his sleeves. But the healing power of merely the tips of his fingers wrought miracles along the way, as he traveled from La Verna to St. Mary of the Angels. One of the many wondrous encounters that took place at this time concerned a woman who came up to the Saint with her young son. The boy had been seriously ill with dropsy for years, and his stomach was so swollen that he could not even see his own legs or feet. The child's mother begged the Saint to pray for him, and he did so while gently caressing the boy's stomach. At the touch of his stigmatized hands, the swelling immediately began to diminish, and the boy was instantly healed.[2]

The Saint continued along his way, encircled by a small group of his friars. They entered a town called Borgo of Sepolcro, since Francis wished to visit a leprosarium that lay on the other side of the village. The little party slowly traversed the city streets, crowded with townspeople who were shouting with joy, waving olive branches and loudly proclaiming, "Here comes the Saint!" They voiced their hosannas to this holy man astride a donkey in a way that was reminiscent of the Saviour's entry into Jerusalem twelve centuries before. The crowds at Borgo repeatedly brushed against Francis in an effort to touch him, and even tore off pieces of his habit. Yet he was completely insensible to the commotion, because the Lord had raised his spirit into an ecstasy, and he was engrossed in contemplating the things of Heaven, not of earth. After they had gone through the city and were approaching the leper colony, Francis came to himself once again. To the amazement of his brother friars, he asked them, "When will we be near Borgo?"[3, 4]

Francis and his brothers arrived that evening at a friary in Monte Casale, and the next morning he sent two of the friars back towards La Verna to return the donkey he had borrowed. On their way there, these brothers passed through a town in the district of Arezzo, where they saw a group of villagers hastening toward them, thinking that Francis was arriving with his friars. They were hoping to ask him to pray for a woman in childbirth who had been in labor for many days, and was in danger of dying because she could not deliver her baby. When they saw that the Saint was not with the group, their hopes began to fade. But, spurred on by their faith in the Poor Man of God, they asked the brothers if they had anything with them that his holy hands had touched. Since the donkey that Francis had ridden still bore the same reins he had handled, the brothers carefully removed the halter and carried it to the bedside of the pregnant woman. There they gently touched to that woman's body the reins that had been in contact with the wounded hands of the Saint, commending her to St. Francis. Although she had already shown signs of death, the woman immediately began to feel better. In a short time she completely recovered and delivered a healthy child without difficulty, to everyone's utter joy and thankfulness.[5]

The last two years in the life of Francis were marked by many signs of God's favor and predilection. Not limited to miracles performed through his intercession, God's grace also extended to allowing him to participate further in the sufferings of Christ. The body of the Poverello was now worn out from his continual fastings, watchings, austerities and constant activity and prayer. His torments were increased by the infirmity of his eyes, which had rendered him nearly blind and caused him such pain that he could barely sleep. He was veritably reduced to a state of skin and bones. At one point, a very innocent and simplistic friar suggested to him that he should beseech God to go easier on him and not treat him so roughly. Francis let out a groan. He replied to that friar that if it were not for his complete simplicity, he would never go near him again, because he had dared to find fault with the way God was treating him. Then Francis threw himself down, and kissing the earth, he thanked God for all of his sufferings. "Nothing would make me more happy than to have you afflict me with pain and not spare me. Doing your will is consolation enough, and more than enough, for me."[6] Francis knew well the secret of the Saints.

During this period of intense agony that accompanied his last years, Francis was no longer able to walk because of the painful nail wounds on his feet. Undaunted, he had the friars carry him to various nearby towns and villages, where he sought to encourage others to endure their own crosses and trials.[7] Although he was scarcely able to move at all, he often repeated, "My brothers, we must begin to serve Our Lord and our God. Until now we have done very little."[8]

For two months he resided near his beloved San Damiano, where Clare and her virgins lived in continual praise of the Lord. A priest and a few friars had been assigned quarters adjacent to the convent, in order to provide for the spiritual needs of the cloistered sisters, and seek alms for their support. These men constructed a tiny hut for Francis next to their abode, which was once the house of the old priest who had assisted in repairing San Damiano years ago. Francis spent nearly all his time in this little cell, afflicted by the cold weather and tormented by Brother Mice, who even climbed over the table while he tried taking his meager meal. Clare and her sisters had the friars bring him medicines they had prepared, hoping to alleviate his eye condition, but the treatment was in vain.

One night, alone in his hut and patiently enduring his tribulations, Francis lifted his spirit to God and prayed for the strength to persevere in carrying his cross—it seemed to be growing too heavy for him to bear. In answer, he heard the Lord speak within his heart, encouraging him to embrace his sufferings and to rejoice and trust in Him, "as if you were already sharing My Kingdom."[9] Francis understood this to be a promise from Christ that he would enter the Heavenly Kingdom upon his death, to enjoy eternal life with his Beloved. The next morning, he jubilantly told his confreres of this most unique and special grace: "He has deigned to assure me, His unworthy servant, of His Kingdom while still living in the flesh."[10]

Francis wished to honor God for this wonderful favor by composing a song in praise of the Giver of all good gifts—a paean in honor of the Most High and the whole of His marvelous creation. And thus was born the immortal "Canticle of Brother Sun," also called the "Canticle of the Creatures." He intended it to be sung, and taught the melody to his brothers. Would that we knew that long-lost refrain today! The Canticle is said to be the oldest known poem in any modern language; it was composed in the Umbrian dialect of the time.[11] Francis also referred to the composition as "The Praises of the Lord." He wished that whenever the friars preached in a town, they would sing the Canticle to the people, as true minstrels of God.

The Canticle of Brother Sun[12]

Most High, Omnipotent, Good Lord,
Thine be the praises, the glory and the honor and
every blessing.

To Thee alone, Most High, do they belong,
and no man is worthy to mention Thee.

May Thou be praised, my Lord, with all Thy
creatures, especially Mister Brother Sun,
of whom is the day, and Thou enlightenest us
through him.

And he is beautiful and radiant with a great
splendor; of Thee, Most High, does he convey the
meaning.

May Thou be praised, my Lord, for Sister Moon
and the stars in Heaven; Thou has made them
clear and precious and beautiful.

May Thou be praised, my Lord, for Brother Wind,
and for the air and the cloudy and the clear
weather and every weather, through which to all
Thy creatures Thou givest sustenance.

May Thou be praised, my Lord, for Sister Water,
who is very useful and humble and precious and
chaste.

May Thou be praised, my lord, for Brother Fire,
through whom Thou illuminest the night,
and he is handsome and jocund and robust and
strong.

May Thou be praised, my Lord, for our sister,
Mother Earth, who sustains us and governs
and produces various fruits with colored flowers
and green plants.

May Thou be praised, my Lord, for those who for-
give for the sake of Thy love and endure infirmity
and tribulation.

Blessed be those who endure them in peace,
because by Thee, Most High, will they be crowned.

May Thou be praised, my Lord, for our sister,
Bodily Death, whom no man living can escape.

Woe to those who die in mortal sin:

blessed are those whom she will find in Thy most
holy desires,
because the second death will do them no evil.

Praise and bless my Lord,
and give Him thanks and serve Him with great
humility!

At the urging of Brother Elias, Francis departed San
Damiano in order to seek medical treatment for his eyes
from doctors at Rieti and Siena. There he underwent primitive and painful procedures that in the end brought little
improvement. As his physical condition weakened, it became
obvious to all that Francis was in his final days, and it was
resolved to bring him to the Bishop's palace at Assisi. Since
the journey to Assisi would take them near Perugia, the
party surreptitiously took a roundabout way to avoid the
town. The reason for such a detour was the very real fear
that the Perugians would forcibly detain the dying Francis
in their city in order to be able to claim his relics at his
death.[13]

He arrived in Assisi in July of 1226 to the great jubilation
of the people, and lodged in the Episcopal palace of Bishop
Guido. The bishop himself was away on a pilgrimage to the
shrine of the Archangel St. Michael, at Monte Sant'Angelo in
the Gargano Mountain of southern Italy.[14] In order to make
sure that their precious heritage remained safely in Assisi,
the citizens posted a round-the-clock guard at the residence.
Francis knew the end was near. He was prepared for death
and welcomed it, since he had a firm hope of attaining
Heaven. His body was quickly fading and weakening, but his
cheerful spirit inspired him to raise his voice in hymns and
songs in praise of God. He sent for Brother Angelo and
Brother Leo and asked them to sing the praises of the Lord

and His creatures by intoning "The Canticle of Brother Sun."
It is believed that on this occasion the Saint composed those
last few verses in praise of "our sister, Bodily Death."[15]
Brother Elias was one of those caring for him. He became
concerned that the guards and others nearby would be scan-
dalized because Francis did not seem penitential and sorrowful in preparation for his imminent death. Francis and
Elias agreed that it would be good to leave the Bishop's
palace, and the Saint asked to be moved to St. Mary of the
Angels, in order to give his soul back to God at his beloved
Portiuncula.[16] And so, accompanied by a great crowd of people, he was borne away on a stretcher and taken outside the
city walls, from which they descended into the valley that led
to St. Mary's.

When they were about halfway there, and near a certain
hospice, Francis was constrained to ask how far they had
come, since his eyesight was almost completely gone. When
told that they had reached the site of this little hospital, he
requested that the litter be set down upon the ground and
turned in the direction of his beloved city of Assisi. Lifting
himself up a little, he solemnly blessed that privileged city
with many inspired and holy words, concluding with: "I
therefore beg Thee, Lord Jesus Christ, Father of Mercies, do
not look upon our ingratitude, but recall to mind the infinite
love that Thou hast shown to this city. May it always remain
the abode and residence of those who will know and glorify
Thy blessed and glorious Name in the ages to come. Amen."[17]
Then, turning him away for the last time from Assisi, the
bearers proceeded to carry St. Francis to the Portiuncula,
where he would spend the final few weeks of his life.

At the same time that Francis was awaiting death at St.
Mary of the Angels, his Sister in Christ, Clare, was herself
seriously ill at her convent in San Damiano. Aware that her
spiritual Father was dying, she became sorrowful at the

thought that she might never see her beloved Francis again
in this life. She sent word of her concern to him via one of the
brothers. Upon receiving the news, Francis sent this brother
back to San Damiano with a blessing for Clare, and with the
message that she and all her sisters would surely behold
him once again, to their great consolation.[18]

On Saturday evening, October 3, 1226, the little poor man
of Assisi, knowing that Sister Death was at hand, asked to be
placed naked on the bare ground. The grieving brothers consented to his wish, and he rested his hand over his chest to
hide its wound from view. Then one of his companions, by
Divine inspiration, loaned him his own tunic, gently placing
it over Francis. This delighted the Saint, for now he was truly
Christ's beggar, clothed in a borrowed habit. He was content
to die in this perfect embrace of Lady Poverty. In the same
way that he had begun his religious life by divesting himself
of his clothing before the bishop, he wished to finish his life
despoiled of everything, in imitation of his crucified Master.[19]

As the final moments drew near, Francis invited the
brothers to come closer and uttered his parting words of
encouragement and consolation, blessing them all. He
entreated them not to abandon the way of poverty, and he
exhorted them to endure patiently the trials and tribulations that the Order would face in the future without him.
Most importantly, he enjoined them to hold fast to the
Gospel and to the faith of Holy Mother Church.[20]

Next he asked them to read from the Thirteenth Chapter
of *John*, which begins with: "Before the festival day of the
pasch, Jesus knowing that his hour was come, that he should
pass out of this world to the Father: having loved his own
who were in the world, he loved them unto the end." (*John*
13:1).[21] Surrounded by his grieving companions, Francis,
who had also loved his own to the end, then gently passed
from this world into the Heavenly Kingdom. His final wish

was that he would be sprinkled with ashes, to symbolize the dust and ashes to which his body would return.[22]

Prodigies and miracles immediately followed upon his death and have continued throughout the centuries to this day. One of the friars, at the moment of Francis' passing, had a vision of the soul of the Saint ascending into Heaven, shining gloriously, borne aloft on a white cloud. Another friar, from a distant town, was close to death himself and had been unable to speak during his final illness. Suddenly he was heard to shout out, "Wait for me, Father. Wait! I am coming with you!" He told the shocked brothers at his bedside that he was addressing Francis, whom he saw rising into Heaven. At that moment he too died.[23] At that same time, Bishop Guido of Assisi, who was still at the Gargano on his pilgrimage to St. Michael's shrine, had a vision of the Saint. A joyful Francis told him that he was happy to be leaving this world for the Heavenly Kingdom of his Beloved Spouse. Upon his return to Assisi, the Bishop was able to verify that Francis had died on the very evening that he had seen this vision.[24]

But the greatest wonder of all was the manifestation of the holy wounds of his stigmata to the brothers who were arriving from afar, and to the citizens of Assisi who were hastening to the Portiuncula. According to St. Bonaventure, "A large number of people from Assisi were admitted to see the stigmata and kiss them."[25] The faith of many laymen and friars was strengthened upon viewing this prodigy, and their sorrow at Francis' passing was converted to astonishment and joy. The next morning a great multitude of the populace, both religious and lay, escorted the body of the Saint to the city of Assisi, amid the singing of hymns and praises of God.

When they neared the convent of St. Clare and her sisters at San Damiano, the entourage stopped and approached the grate where the cloistered nuns were wont to receive Holy

Communion from the priests. The iron grille was removed, and Francis' body was lifted so that Clare and her spiritual family could venerate the holy wounds of their Father. Thus was fulfilled the prophecy of the dying Francis, who had sent word to Clare that she and her sisters would behold him once again.[26]

The procession then made its way into the town, and the remains of the beloved Poverello were laid to rest in the Church of San Giorgio, the same church in which Clare had first heard him preach. He had died in the forty-fifth year of his life, and the twentieth since his spiritual conversion in 1206, having borne the stigmata for two years.

On July 16, 1228, Pope Gregory IX came to San Giorgio in Assisi and canonized St. Francis—not quite two years after he had died! The next day the Holy Father laid the cornerstone for the great new Basilica that would honor St. Francis and permanently house his remains. Two years later his body was secretly buried deep beneath the altar in the church crypt. It remained hidden there for six hundred years until it was found in 1818.[27]

The ritual of the *Transitus*, or the passing of Francis from death to eternal life, is enacted by Franciscans every year on the evening of October 3. Although he actually passed away on that date, the feast day of St. Francis is celebrated throughout the Christian world on October 4.

Conclusion

St. Francis and the Sultan

AS promised in the Introduction, this concluding chapter will consider whether or not Francis was successful in his efforts to convert the Sultan of Egypt to the True Faith. Arguments can be made for either thesis: that Sultan al-Malik al-Kamil was ultimately converted to the Christian Religion or that he remained loyal to Islam. Although Francis was the primary source of al-Kamil's exposure to Christianity, he was actually not the only person to try to convert him. Two years after the meetings between Francis and the Sultan, one of the Crusaders, Oliver of Paderborn, wrote a letter to al-Kamil in which he tried to persuade him to become a Christian. Paderborn had been taken prisoner by the Muslims after the debacle of the Fifth Crusade, and wrote the letter after his release. In it he attempted to convince the Sultan to convert by using theological arguments largely from the Old Testament, which he mistakenly thought that Muslims accepted.[1]

The story from the *Little Flowers* told above in Chapter 12 about the Sultan's deathbed conversion might read like a pious fable, but it is quite possibly based on a real incident. As mentioned in that chapter, the story is taken from ancient Franciscan sources which are not merely folklore, but have a "definite historical value."[2] Franciscanism was in full flower in the century following its founder's passing. Thus, there is no reason to believe that friars who either knew Francis or who lived shortly after his death would intentionally

126

embellish the chronicles of the Order to the extent of completely fabricating an event.

Because of his efforts, it is certain that the preaching of Francis did have an influence on the Sultan. In fact, the context of his entire visit reflects the amazing working of grace. The Sultan had it in his power to have Francis executed by beheading, as his advisors, the *imams*, implored him to do in the name of Islamic law. If Francis had died at this period of his life, which was before he had finalized the Rule and received the stigmata, it is quite possible the Order would have foundered. We have seen that during his stay in the Middle East, serious problems and division in the Order had already begun to erupt. But the Providence of God willed otherwise.

Although their visit took place during a period of truce, Francis and Illuminato had arrived as Christian missionaries, rather than as emissaries of the Crusaders. Thus there was no political reason to spare these infidel friars, who dared to try to draw the Sultan and his court away from the worship of Allah. Furthermore, Sultan al-Kamil could have viewed their bold preaching of Christianity as an insult and affront to the dignity and pride of the conquerors of the Crusaders in the recently fought battle at Damietta. But the power of the Saint's preaching in the name of Jesus, and the love that was manifested by his desire for the salvation of al-Kamil, moved the Sultan to spare the lives of the Poverello and his companion.

Francis made such an impact on the Sultan that it seems a friendship based on mutual respect had developed between them. Not only did Francis survive the danger of being martyred, but he succeeded in actually pleasing the Sultan, who enjoyed hearing him and being in his presence. During the prolonged visit, which might have lasted a number of weeks, al-Kamil often sent for Francis to appear before him.

However, it is of crucial importance to emphasize that Francis visited the Sultan for the purpose of converting him to the Christian Religion, not to engage in a friendly dialogue in order to establish a non-belligerent tolerance of the two parties for each other's religion. Francis was able to sustain this friendship while engaging in his conversion-oriented talks, even despite his sharp and blunt statements that Islam was not the true religion and therefore could not bring eternal life to its followers.

Such success was of course due to grace. But on the visible level, it could only be due to the positive aspects of Francis' preaching, in which he became the face of Christianity to the Muslims. This face of Francis, this *persona Christi* of sorts, reflected the depth of his own Christian spirituality. In short, Francis was the presence of Christ to the Sultan. The Christian virtues that shone forth from him—his love, compassion, kindness and mercy, plus his concern for the soul of the Sultan—were the heart of his Christianity. This love was joined to his openness, candidness and his simple Franciscan humility. A work attributed to some of the first followers of St. Francis describes his holy simplicity: "He spoke from the fervor of his heart, for he had been chosen by God to be simple and unlearned, using none of the erudite words of human wisdom, and in all things he bore himself with simplicity."[3]

St. Francis was bold yet gentle. His gentleness and Christian meekness were not timid or cowardly and did not cause him to draw back and shrink before the threatening situation, especially during his initial encounters with the sentries and the hostile *imams*. His confidence and fearlessness reflected the action of the Holy Spirit. The Spirit inspired his zeal and emboldened him to overcome human weakness. Pope Gregory IX, in the Bull of Canonization of the Saint, wrote that Francis conquered "by his simple preaching, unadorned with the persuasive words of human wisdom and made forceful by the power of God, who chooses the weak of this world to confound the strong."[4] What then was the specific content of his preaching that caused it to make such an impact on the Sultan? The Franciscan Rule is the key that reveals the substance of Francis' preaching. Chapter XVI of the Rule of 1221, regarding the mission to the unbelievers, was in all likelihood written soon after his return from Egypt, as noted previously (Chapter 13). In it he declares that the friars, when they have seen that it is pleasing to the Lord, are to "announce the word of God." This is the very first teaching precept that he mentions. And to what purpose is the word of God announced? That the infidels and Saracens may believe in the Triune God and in Jesus the Redeemer, in order to be baptized and become Christians. Essentially, Francis was presenting Jesus as a Divine Person and the Saviour of mankind, rather than as just another prophet who was no different from the prophets who had come before Him, as the *Koran* teaches. (*Koran* 2:136).

St. Francis was completely loyal to the Catholic Church and its beliefs, hierarchy, priesthood and sacraments. The Appendix presents the statement of Pope Pius XI from 1926, criticizing those who even at that time were trying to portray the Saint as opposed to Church authority and discipline. However, from what is known about the content of his preaching to the Muslims, he did not appear to be expounding on the nature and structure of the Catholic Church as such, nor was he asking them to consent to a long list of required beliefs and ceremonies. He was simply preaching the Gospel, and a Person—Jesus Christ. In essence, he was confessing his belief in Jesus, as it states in the very next line in Chapter XVI of the Rule: "Every man, who confesses Me before men, him I will confess also before My Father, who is in Heaven." (*Matthew* 10:32).

Francis had an apostolic understanding and awareness of

Jesus Christ—his knowledge of and love for Christ were based on actual encounters with Him. Even before the Lord spoke to him through the San Damiano crucifix, He had voiced His will to him in dreams. For Francis, the road to Mount La Verna, his own Calvary, was paved with many visions and heavenly communications from Our Lord.

Thus, for the Poverello, preaching Christianity meant preaching Jesus Christ, because the Divine Head of the Church is a Person. (*Colossians* 1:18). This is nothing novel. When Saul, the future Apostle Paul, drew nigh to Damascus, "breathing out threatenings and slaughter against the disciples of the Lord," Jesus said to him, "Saul, Saul, why persecutest thou Me?" (Cf. *Acts* 9:1-4). Here Our Lord identified Himself with His disciples and His Church. By persecuting the budding Church, Saul was persecuting Jesus Christ Himself.

In the words of Fortini, "He fought in the Crusade, in which he and he alone emerged the victor."[5] At the very least, Francis profoundly influenced the Sultan and perhaps even effected his conversion. The simple approach of Francis, with its focus on the Person of Jesus and His Divinity, might be the answer to the common lament even today that converting the Muslims is such a difficult task. "Too often one hears repeated by the very persons who live in the lands of Islam: 'There is nothing that can be done!' How many times, in the course of seventeen years spent in Muslim territory, have I heard my own confreres enunciate this sad conclusion."[6] Thus wrote a Friar Minor of the twentieth century.

The Christian Religion is meant to encompass all peoples, races and nations. Christ's great commission to His followers is to preach the Gospel to all creatures, baptizing them in the name of the Father, the Son, and the Holy Spirit. This is what motivated Francis to go out among the unbelievers, and it is the only option for the followers of Christ. "And Jesus coming, spoke to them, saying: All power is given to Me in heaven and in earth. Going therefore, teach ye all nations, baptizing them in the name of the Father and of the Son and of the Holy Ghost, teaching them to observe all things whatsoever I have commanded you; and behold I am with you all days, even to the consummation of the world." (*Matthew* 28:18-20).

The mission of St. Francis must be ongoing and must continue, because at the very beginning of his calling he was charged by Christ to rebuild the Church: "Francis, go, repair My house, which, as you see, is falling completely to ruin." Christianity is the house that Christ built. Yet, today more than ever, Christendom is divided and in ruins. There is no need or desire here to expound upon the long and obvious list of problems, which range from today's apparent triumph of secularism, to tomorrow's possible ascendancy of Islam.

Although the question of whether or not Sultan al-Kamil was converted cannot be answered definitively, I personally believe that Francis was successful in his efforts to do so. It is quite possible that this conversion took place in al-Kamil's heart during the time of Francis' visit in the Fifth Crusade. However, the Sultan's newborn faith might not have been strong enough for him to face the prospect of the immediate martyrdom that would befall him if he were baptized at that time. Of course, none of this can be proved, and it would be a vain effort to try to prove the unprovable. But one thing is certain. We know that Francis *tried*. If Francis had not at least made the effort to convert al-Kamil, we would not even be asking the question of whether or not he was successful. This is why the tale of St. Francis and the Sultan lives on— because the Saint made the attempt, at the risk of his life, to save the soul of the Sultan. It is this noble endeavor that is the true legacy of the Franciscans, and of all Christendom.

Appendix

Statement of Pope Pius XI in 1926

"WHAT evil they do and how far from a true appreciation of the Man of Assisi are they who, in order to bolster up their fantastic and erroneous ideas about him, imagine such an incredible thing as that Francis was an opponent of the discipline of the Church, that he did not accept the dogmas of the Faith, that he was the precursor and prophet of that false liberty which began to manifest itself at the beginning of modern times and which has caused so many disturbances both in the Church and in civil society! That he was in a special manner obedient and faithful in all things to the hierarchy of the Church, to this Apostolic See, and to the teachings of Christ, the 'Herald of the Great King' proved both to Catholics and non-Catholics by the admirable example of obedience, which he always gave. It is a fact proven by contemporary documents, which are worthy of all credence, 'that he held in veneration the clergy and loved with a great affection all who were in Holy Orders.' (Thomas of Celano, *Legenda*, Chap. I, No. 62). 'As a man who was truly Catholic and apostolic, he insisted above all things in his sermons that the faith of the Holy Roman Church should always be preserved, and inviolably, and that the priests who by their ministry bring into being the sublime Sacrament of the Lord, should therefore be held in the highest reverence. He also taught that the doctors of the law of God and all the orders of clergy should be

shown the utmost respect at all times.' (Julian a Spira, *Life of St. Francis*, No. 28). That which he taught to the people from the pulpit he insisted on much more strongly among his friars. We may read of this in his famous last testament, and again at the very point of death, he admonished them about this with great insistence, namely, that in the exercise of the sacred ministry, they should always obey the bishops and the clergy and should live together with them, as it behooves children of peace." —Pope Pius XI
Rite Expiatis, No. 23*

---

* http://www.vatican.va/holy_father/pius_xi/encyclicals/documents/hf_p-xi_enc_30041926_rite-expiatis_en.html.

Chapter Notes

Introduction

1. Pope Pius XI, *Rite Expiatis,* no. 3, http://www.vatican.va/holy_father /pius_xi/encyclicals/documents/hf_p-xi_enc_30041926_rite-expiatis _en.html.
2. Arnaldo Fortini, *Nova Vita di San Francesco,* Roma, Carucci Editore, 1981.
3. J. Hoeberichts, *Francis and Islam,* Quincy, IL, Franciscan Press, 1997, p. xi.
4. *Ibid.,* p. 86.
5. *Ibid.,* p. 133.
6. *Ibid.,* p. 134.
7. *Ibid.,* p. ix, Foreword by Terrence J. Riddell, Director, Franciscan Press.
8. *Ibid.,* p. 75.
9. Benjamin Z. Kedar, *Crusade and Mission: European Approaches toward the Muslims,* Princeton, Princeton University Press, 1984.
10. *Ibid.,* p. 125.
11. St. Bonaventure, *Major Life of St. Francis,* Tr. by Benen Fahy, O.F.M., included in *St. Francis of Assisi: Writings and Early Biographies, English Omnibus of Sources for the Life of St. Francis* (hereafter identified as *Omnibus*), Marion A. Habig, Editor, Chicago, Franciscan Herald Press, 1973, Third Revised Edition, Chapter IX, no. 4, p. 700.
12. Hoeberichts, p. 196.

Chapter 1.
YOUTHFUL DREAMS OF KNIGHTHOOD

1. Thomas of Celano, *The Second Life of St. Francis, Book One,* Tr. by Placid Hermann, O.F.M., Chapter 1, no. 3; p. 363, *Omnibus.*
2. St. Bonaventure, *Major Life,* Chapter 1, no. 1; pp. 635-636, *Omnibus.*
3. *Legend of the Three Companions,* Tr. by Nesta de Robeck, Chapter 1, no. 3; p. 892, *Omnibus.*
4. *Ibid.,* p. 893.
5. Celano, *Second Life, Book One,* Chapter 2, no. 5; p. 365, *Omnibus.*
6. Thomas of Celano, *The First Life of St. Francis, Book One,* Tr. by Placid Hermann, O.F.M., Book I, footnote no. 20; p. 563, *Omnibus.*

7. St. Bonaventure, *Major Life*, Chapter 1, no. 3; p. 637, *Omnibus*.
8. Celano, *Second Life, Book One*, Chapter 3, no. 7; p. 367, *Omnibus*.
9. *Three Companions*, Chapter 5, no. 13; p. 903, *Omnibus*.
10. *Ibid.*, Chapter IV, no. 11; p. 900, *Omnibus*.
11. "Leprosy" (2007), in *Encyclopædia Britannica*. Retrieved February 23, 2007, from Encyclopædia Britannica Online:http://www.britannica.com/eb/article-248485.
12. *The Testament of St. Francis*, Tr. by Benen Fahy, O.F.M.; p. 67, *Omnibus*.

Chapter 2.
"FRANCIS, GO, REPAIR MY HOUSE"

1. The history and meaning of the San Damiano crucifix is explained at various web sites such as: The Story of the Cross, http://www.poorclarestmd.org/cross.htm, and The Story of the San Damiano Crucifix, http://www.monasteryicons.com/info/san_damiano_cross.hzml.
2. Celano, *Second Life, Book One*, Chapter 6, no. 10; p. 370, *Omnibus*.
3. *Three Companions*, Chapter 6, no. 19; p. 908, *Omnibus*.
4. Celano, *Second Life, Book One*, Chapter 7, no. 12; p. 372, *Omnibus*.
5. *Three Companions*, Chapter 6, no. 20; p. 909, *Omnibus*.
6. St. Bonaventure, *Major Life*, Chapter 2, no. 4; p. 643, *Omnibus*.

Chapter 3.
HERALD OF THE GREAT KING

1. St. Bonaventure, *Major Life*, Chapter 2, no. 5; p. 643, *Omnibus*.
2. Omer Englebert and Raphael Brown, *Chronology*; p. xi, *Omnibus*.
3. Celano, *Second Life, Book One*, Chapter 8, no. 13; p. 373, *Omnibus*.
4. Celano, *First Life, Book One*, Chapter 8, no. 18; p. 244, *Omnibus*.
5. St. Clare of Assisi, *Testament*, translated from the Latin by Brother Alexis Bugnolo, Editor of "The Franciscan Archive, A WWW Resource on St. Francis & Franciscanism," http://www.franciscan-archive.org/; used with permission.
6. "Portiuncula," by Michael Bihl, in *The Catholic Encyclopedia*, Vol. XII, 1911, p. 286, courtesy of Kevin Knight's New Advent website: http://www.newadent.org/cathen/12286a.htm.
7. St. Bonaventure, *Major Life*, Chapter 2, no. 8; p. 646, *Omnibus*.
8. Fortini, footnote no. 2, p. 317.
9. Celano, *First Life, Book One*, Chapter 9, no. 22; p. 247, *Omnibus*.

10. Celano, *Second Life, Book One,* Chapter 10, no. 15; p. 375, *Omnibus.*
11. St. Bonaventure, *Major Life,* Chapter 3, no. 3; p. 647-648, *Omnibus.*

Chapter 4.
"THE LESSER BROTHERS"

1. Celano, *Second Life, Book Two,* Chapter 151, no. 200; p. 522, *Omnibus.*
2. Fr. Candide Chalippe, O.F.M., *The Life and Legends of Saint Francis of Assisi,* revised and re-edited by Fr. Hilarion Duerk, O.F.M., New York, P.J. Kenedy & Sons, 1918, p. 59.
3. *Three Companions,* Chapter 9, no. 35; p. 923, *Omnibus.*
4. St. Bonaventure, *Major Life,* Chapter 3, no. 9; p. 651, *Omnibus.*
5. "Albigenses," by N. A. Weber, *The Catholic Encyclopedia,* Vol. I, 1907, p. 267, http://www.newadvent.org/cathen/01267e.htm.
6. Fortini, pp. 375-376.
7. St. Bonaventure, *Major Life,* Chapter 3, no. 9; p. 652, *Omnibus.*
8. *The Rule of 1221,* Tr. by Benen Fahy, O.F.M., Introduction and notes by Placid Hermann, O.F.M., footnote no. 7; p. 28, *Omnibus.*

Chapter 5.
RIVO TORTO

1. *The Rule of 1223,* Tr. by Benen Fahy, O.F.M., Introduction and notes by Placid Hermann, O.F.M., Chapter 9; p. 63, *Omnibus.*
2. St. Bonaventure, *Major Life,* Chapter 4, no. 3; p. 655, *Omnibus.*
3. *The Testament of St. Francis,* p. 67, *Omnibus.*
4. *Ibid.*
5. Celano, *First Life, Book One,* Chapter 18, no. 47; pp. 268-269, *Omnibus.*
6. St. Bonaventure, *Major Life,* Chapter 4, no. 4; pp. 655-656, *Omnibus.*
7. *Legend of Perugia,* Tr. by Paul Oligny, no. 9; p. 985, *Omnibus.*

Chapter 6.
THE FIRST FLOWER

1. Celano, *First Life, Book One,* Chapter 8, no. 18; p. 244, *Omnibus.*
2. St. Bonaventure, *Major Life,* Chapter 4, no. 6; p. 657, *Omnibus.*
3. *The Life of St. Clare Virgin,* Fra' Tommaso da Celano, Tr. by Catherine

Bolton Magrini, Assisi, Editrice Minerva, 2001, p. 18, footnote no. 15.

4. *Ibid.*, p. 23.
5. *Ibid.*, p. 24.
6. *Ibid.*, pp. 48-51.
7. See note 3 above.
8. *Ibid.*, p. 44.
9. *Ibid.*, p. 45.

Chapter 7.
BEARERS OF PEACE

1. *Little Flowers of St. Francis*, Tr. by Raphael Brown, Chapter 16; p. 1334, *Omnibus*.
2. *Ibid.*, p. 1335.
3. Celano, *First Life, Book One*, Chapter 29, no. 81; p. 297, *Omnibus*.
4. *Ibid.*,Chapter 21, no. 59; pp. 278-279, *Omnibus*.
5. St. Bonaventure, *Major Life*, Chapter 12, no. 4; p. 723, *Omnibus*.
6. *Little Flowers*, Chapter 16; p. 1335, *Omnibus*.
7. St. Bonaventure, *Major Life*, Chapter 12, no. 4; p. 723, *Omnibus*.
8. *Little Flowers*, Chapter 16; pp. 1335-1336, *Omnibus*.
9. Fortini, pp. 663-669.
10. The Church of S. Francesco in Cannara, http://penelope.uchicago. edu/Thayer/E/Gazetteer/Places/Europe/Italy/Umbria/Perugia/Can nara/Cannara/churches/S.Francesco/home.html.
11. *The Rule of the Third Order,* Tr. by Benen Fahy, O.F.M., Introduction and notes by Placid Hermann, O.F.M., p. 167, *Omnibus*.
12. Marion A. Habig, O.F.M., and Mark Hegener, O.F.M., *A Short History of the Third Order,* Chicago, Franciscan Herald Press, Revised Edition, 1977, pp. 18-19.
13. *Ibid.*, Chapter V, no. 16; p. 171.
14. Rule and Form of Life of the Brothers and Sisters of Penance, http:// www.franciscan-sfo.org/Rule1289.htm, section 7.
15. The Rule of the Secular Franciscan Order, http://www.franciscan -sfo.org/ FFMR/Rule.htm, Chapter 2, no. 19.
16. *The Rule of the Third Order,* Chapter V, no. 17; p. 171, *Omnibus*.
17. Historical Outline, The Secular Franciscan Order, http://www. franciscan-sfo.org/history2.htm.
18. "Franciscan Nonviolence," http://www.ofm-jpic.org/peace/nonviolence /nonviolence_en.pdf, pp. 12, 20.

19. "Third Orders," by Bede Jarrett et al., in *The Catholic Encyclopedia*, Vol. XIV, 1912, p. 637, http:// www.newadvent.org/cathen/14637b.htm.

20. Fortini, p. 465.

21. Chalippe, p. 82.

Chapter 8.
MISSIONARY JOURNEY TO THE MIDDLE EAST

1. Sezzi, Linda, *San Francesco alla corte del sultano. Fallimento del dialogo interreligioso all'alba del XIII secolo?* Thesis, University of Bologna, 2002-2003; http://www.tesionline.com/intl/thesis.jsp?idt =9362, page 101.

2. Celano, *First Life, Book One*, Chapter 20, no. 55, footnote no. 181; page 573, *Omnibus*.

3. *Ibid.*, page 275.

4. *Ibid.*

5. Martiniano Roncaglia, *St. Francis of Assisi and the Middle East*, Tr. by Stephen A. Janto, O.F.M., Franciscan Center of Oriental Studies, Cairo, 1954, p. 26.

6. St. Bonaventure, *Major Life*, Chapter 9, no. 6; p. 702, *Omnibus*.

7. Franciscan Custody of the Holy Land, http://www.christusrex. org/www1/ofm/cust/TShistry.html.

8. Roncaglia, p. 21.

9. "Elias of Cortona." by Paschal Robinson, in *The Catholic Encyclopedia*, Vol. V, 1909, p. 286, http://www.newadvent.org/cathen/05382a.htm.

10. Fortini, pp. 496-497.

11. Dante Alighieri, *The Divine Comedy: Paradiso*, Tr. by Rev. H. F. Cary, M.A., Canto XII, v. 130-132, http://www.gutenberg.org/etext/8800.

12. *Little Flowers*, Chapter 24; footnote no. 3; p. 1519, *Omnibus*.

13. *A New Fioretti*, Tr. by John R. H. Moorman, D.D., Chapter 54; p. 1878, *Omnibus*.

14. Celano, *Second Life, Book Two*, Chapter 4, no. 30, footnote no. 11; p. 589, *Omnibus*.

Chapter 9.
THE TRAGIC BATTLE OF DAMIETTA

1. "Damietta" (2007), in *Encyclopædia Britannica*. Retrieved February 26, 2007, from Encyclopædia Britannica Online:

http://www.britannica.com/eb/article-9028650.
2. Fortini, pp. 499-500.
3. James M. Powell, *Anatomy of a Crusade, 1213-1221*, Philadelphia, University of Pennsylvania Press, 1986, p. 178.
4. E. L. Skip Knox, *The Fifth Crusade*, Boise State University online course, http://Crusades.boisestate.edu/5th/04.shtml.
5. *Ibid.*, http://crusades.boisestate.edu/5th/06.shtml.
6. Powell, *Anatomy of a Crusade*, p. 158.
7. Fortini, p. 514.
8. *Ibid.*, p. 512.
9. St. Bonaventure, *Major Life*, Chapter 11, no. 3; p. 713, *Omnibus*.
10. Celano, *Second Life, Book Two*, Chapter 4, no. 30; p. 388, *Omnibus*.
11. Fortini, pp. 514-516.
12. Powell, *Anatomy of a Crusade*, pp. 158-159.
13. Celano, *Second Life, Book Two*, Chapter 4, no. 30; p. 389, *Omnibus*.
14. Alberto Milioli, *Gesta obsidionis Damiatae, mai*, p. 1098, cited in Fortini, footnote no. 3, p. 517.
15. Celano, *Second Life, Book Two*, Chapter 4, no. 30; p. 389, *Omnibus*.
16. St. Bonaventure, *Major Life*, Chapter 11, no. 3; p. 713, *Omnibus*.
17. Milioli, *Gesta,* p. 1098, cited in Fortini, footnote no. 5, p. 517.
18. Kedar, p. 158.

Chapter 10.
FACE TO FACE WITH THE SULTAN

1. Roncaglia, p. 27.
2. St. Bonaventure, *Major Life*, Chapter 9, no. 7; p. 703, *Omnibus*.
3. Powell, *Anatomy of a Crusade*, p. 159.
4. St. Bonaventure, *Major Life*, Chapter 9, no. 8; p. 703, *Omnibus*.
5. Herbert J. Thurston, S.J., and Donald Attwater, Editors, *Butler's Lives of the Saints*, Volume IV, October 4, "St. Francis of Assisi, Founder of the Friars Minor," Westminster, Maryland, Christian Classics, 1987, p. 28.
6. Sezzi, p. 111.
7. Jacques de Vitry, *History of the Orient*, Chapter 32, quoted in Chalippe, p. 169.
8. Celano, *First Life, Book One*, Chapter 20, no. 57; p. 277, *Omnibus*.
9. St. Bonaventure, *Major Life*, Chapter 9, no. 8; p. 703, *Omnibus*.
10. Jacques de Vitry, *History of the Orient*, Chapter 32; p. 1612, *Omnibus*.
11. Roncaglia, footnote no. 52, p. 28.

12. Fortini, p. 547.
13. Jacques de Vitry, *History of the Orient*, Chapter 32; p. 1612, *Omnibus*.
14. Sezzi, p. 111.
15. *Ibid.*, p. 101.
16. Three Translations of The Koran (Al-Qur'an), http://www.gutenberg. org/files/16955/16955.txt, Tr. by Abdullah Yusuf Ali.
17. Celano, *First Life, Book One*, Chapter 20, no. 57; p. 276, *Omnibus*.
18. St. Bonaventure, *Major Life*, Chapter 9, no. 8; pp. 703-704, *Omnibus*.
19. Ernoul, *Cronaca di Ernoul e di Bernardo il Tesoriere*, quoted in Sezzi, p. 105, present author's translation.
20. *Ibid.*
21. Powell, *Anatomy of a Crusade*, p. 159.
22. Christoph T. Maier, *Preaching the Crusades: Mendicant Friars and the Cross in the Thirteenth Century*, Cambridge, U.K., Cambridge University Press, 1994, p. 11.
23. Fortini, p. 548.
24. Ernoul, *Cronaca di Ernoul e di Bernardo il Tesoriere*, quoted in Sezzi, p. 116, present author's translation.
25. Jacques de Vitry, *Letter, 1220*; p. 1609, *Omnibus*.
26. Sezzi, p. 111.
27. "Francis of Assisi, Saint" (2007), in *Encyclopædia Britannica*. Retrieved February 28, 2007, from Encyclopædia Britannica Online: http://www.britannica.com/eb/article-2422.
28. Jacques de Vitry, *History of the Orient*, Chapter 32; p. 1612, *Omnibus*.
29. *Little Flowers*, Chapter 24, footnote no. 3; p. 1519, *Omnibus*.
30. Sezzi, p. 112.
31. Three Translations of The Koran (Al-Qur'an), http://www.gutenberg. org/files/16955/16955.txt, Tr. by Mohammad Habib Shakir.
32. Roncaglia, footnote no. 46, p. 26.
33. *Ibid.*, footnote 54, p. 28.
34. "Sufism" (2007), in *Encyclopædia Britannica*. Retrieved February 28, 2007, from Encyclopædia Britannica Online: http://www.britannica. com/eb/article-68905.
35. James M. Powell, "*Francesco d'Assisi e la Quinta Crociata, Una Missione di Pace,*" in *Schede Medievali*, 4 (1983), p. 75.
36. Maier, pp. 16-17.

Chapter 11.
TRIAL BY FIRE

1. St. Bonaventure, *Excerpts from Other Works,* Tr. by Benen Fahy, O.F.M., no. 3; p. 838, *Omnibus.*
2. St. Bonaventure, *Major Life,* Chapter 9, no. 8; p. 704, *Omnibus.*
3. St. Bonaventure, *Excerpts,* no. 3; p. 839, *Omnibus.*
4. Anonymous, *St. Francis and the Sultan of Egypt, Thirteenth-Century Testimonies,* Tr. by Paul Oligny O.F.M., no. 13; p. 1614, *Omnibus.*
5. *Ibid.*
6. *Ms. Vatican, Biblioteca Apostolica, Ottob. Lat. 522, f.243r(92r),* footnote no. 19, cited in Maier, p. 14.
7. Powell, *Anatomy of a Crusade,* p. 143.
8. Maier, p. 14.
9. Knox, E. L. Skip, *The Fifth Crusade,* Boise State University online course, http://crusades.boisestate.edu/5th/13.shtml.
10. Rengers, Christopher, O.F.M. Cap., Capuchin Franciscan Friars, Province of St. Augustine, http://www.capuchin.com/index.php?page=home.
11. Fortini, p. 552.
12. Anonymous, *St. Francis and the Sultan of Egypt,* no. 13; p. 1615, *Omnibus.*
13. *Ibid.*
14. Powell, James M., *St. Francis of Assisi's way of Peace,* manuscript copy made available to the present author, courtesy of Professor Powell. The article will be published in a forthcoming edition of the journal "Medieval Encounters," published by Brill, http://www.brill.nl.
15. Maier, p. 16.
16. *Legend of Perugia,* Tr. by Paul Oligny, no. 72; pp. 1048-1049, *Omnibus.*
17. Celano, *First Life, Book One,* Chapter 20, no. 57; p. 277, *Omnibus.*
18. St. Bonaventure, *Major Life,* Chapter 9, no. 8; pp. 704-705, *Omnibus.*
19. Celano, *First Life, Book One,* Chapter 20, no. 57; p. 277, *Omnibus.*

Chapter 12.
DEATHBED CONVERSION?

1. Fortini, p. 553.
2. Jacques de Vitry, *History of the Orient,* Chapter 32; p. 1612, *Omnibus.*
3. Celano, *First Life, Book One,* Chapter 20, no. 57; p. 277, *Omnibus.*
4. Jacques de Vitry, *History of the Orient,* Chapter 32; p. 1612, *Omnibus.*

5. *Little Flowers*, Chapter 24, footnote no. 3; p. 1519, *Omnibus*.
6. Fortini, p. 554.
7. Official Web Site of the Basilica and Sacred Convent of St. Francis in Assisi, http://www.sanfrancescoassisi.org/.
8. *Ibid.*
9. "Aziz's Assisi praise for marchers," CNN Web Site, http://www.cnn.com/2003/WORLD/meast/02/15/sprj.irq.aziz.assisi.1330/index.html?e ref=sitesearch.
10. Fortini, footnote no. 3, pp. 554-555.
11. *Little Flowers*, Chapter 24; p. 1354, *Omnibus*.
12. *Legend of Perugia*, no. 37; p. 1015, *Omnibus*.
13. St. Bonaventure, *Major Life*, Chapter 5, no. 8; p. 668, *Omnibus*.
14. Fortini, p. 553.
15. Powell, *"Francesco d'Assisi e la Quinta Crociata,"* p. 71.
16. Dante, *The Divine Comedy: Paradiso*, Canto XI, v. 100-105, http://www.gutenberg.org/etext/8800.
17. Powell, *Anatomy of a Crusade*, p. 191.
18. *Little Flowers*, Chapter 24, footnote no. 3; p. 1519, *Omnibus*.
19. *Ibid.*, "Introduction," p. 1283.
20. *Ibid.*, Chapter 24, p. 1355.
21. *Ibid.*, p. 1356.
22. Chalippe, pp. 173-174.
23. Jacques de Vitry, *History of the Orient,* cited in Sezzi, p. 116.
24. Oliviero da Colonia, *Epistola salutaris regi Babilonis,* quoted in Sezzi, p. 117, present author's translation.
25. Roncaglia, p. 41.

Chapter 13.
THE RULE OF 1221

1. *Chronology*; p. xiii, *Omnibus*.
2. Fortini, p. 558.
3. Celano, *First Life, Book One*, Chapter 20, no. 57, footnote no. 191; pp. 573-574, *Omnibus*.
4. *Ibid.*
5. Roncaglia, p. 30.
6. *The Rule of 1221*, Tr. by Benen Fahy, O.F.M., Introduction and notes by Placid Hermann, O.F.M., footnote no. 7, p. 28, *Omnibus*.
7. *Ibid.*, pp. 30-31.

8. "The Franciscan Experience, 2. Writings of St. Francis of Assisi," http://www.christusrex.org/www1/ofm/fra/FRAwr03.html.
9. Hoeberichts, p 47.
10. Serge Trifkovic, *The Sword of the Prophet,* Boston, Regina Orthodox Press, Inc., 2002, pp. 103-109.
11. Robert Spencer, *The Politically Incorrect Guide to Islam (and the Crusades),* Washington, D.C., Regnery Publishing, Inc., 2005, pp. 49-54.
12. "The Dhimmi: an Overview," http://www.dhimmi.com/dhimmi_overview.htm.
13. "jizya" (2007), in *Encyclopædia Britannica.* Retrieved March 12, 2007, from Encyclopædia Britannica Online: http://www.britannica.com/eb/article-9043677.
14. Hilaire Belloc, "The Great and Enduring Heresy of Mohammed," originally from *The Great Heresies* in *Moslems: Their Beliefs, Practices and Politics,* Ridgefield, CT., Roger A. McCaffrey Publishing, 2002, p. 107.
15. "The Writings of St. Francis of Assisi," *The Regula Bullata,* Translated from Critical Latin Edition of Fr. Kajetan Esser, O.F.M., by Brother Alexis Bugnolo, Editor of the Franciscan Archive,http://www.franciscan-archive.org/patriarcha/opera/rules.html; used with permission.
16. Francis Borgia Steck, O.F.M., *Glories of the Franciscan Order,* Chicago, Franciscan Herald Press, 1926, p. 49.
17. Marion A. Habig, O.F.M., *In Journeyings Often,* New York, The Franciscan Institute, 1953, p. 196.
18. "The Writings of St. Francis of Assisi," *The Regula non Bullata,* Translated from Critical Latin Edition of Fr. Kajetan Esser, O.F.M., by Brother Alexis Bugnolo, Editor of the Franciscan Archive,http://www.franciscan-archive.org/patriarcha/opera/rules.html; used with permission.

Chapter 14.
THE FIRST FRANCISCAN MARTYRS

1. Jacques de Vitry, *History of the Orient,* Chapter 32; pp. 1612-1613, *Omnibus.*
2. Fortini, p. 491.
3. Chalippe, p. 154.
4. Celano, *Second Life, Book Two,* Chapter 158, no. 208; p. 528, *Omnibus.*
5. Chalippe, p. 161.
6. *Ibid.*

7. *Ibid.,* p. 162.
8. Fortini, p. 492.
9. Chalippe, p. 192.
10. John V. Tolan, *Saracens: Islam in the medieval European Imagination*, New York, Columbia University Press, 2002, pp. 216-217.
11. Chalippe, p. 193.
12. Sezzi, p. 113, present author's translation.
13. Marion A. Habig, O.F.M., *The Franciscan Book of Saints*, Chicago, Franciscan Herald Press, 1959, p. 34.
14. "St. Anthony of Padua," by Nicolaus Del-Gal, in *The Catholic Encyclopedia*, Vol. I, 1907, p. 556, http://www.newadvent.org/cathen/01556 a.htm.
15. Official Portal of St. Anthony of Padua, http://www.saintanthony ofpadua.net/portale/home.asp.
16. *Butler's Lives of the Saints*, Volume I, January 16, "SS. Berard and his Companions, Martyrs," p. 103.
17. *Chronicle of Jordan,* quoted in Hoeberichts, p. 74.
18. Giordano da Giano, cited in Sezzi, p. 113.
19. *The Admonitions,* Tr. by Benen Fahy, O.F.M., Introduction and notes by Placid Hermann, O.F.M., no. 6; p. 81, *Omnibus.*
20. *Legend of Perugia,* Tr. by Paul Oligny, no. 72; pp. 1048-1049, *Omnibus.*
21. Hoeberichts, p. 87.
22. *Legend of Perugia, Introduction*, Theophile Desbonnets, Tr. by Paul Oligny; pp. 959-971, *Omnibus.*
23. Jacques de Vitry, *History of the Orient,* Chapter 32; pp. 1612-1613, *Omnibus.*
24. Hoeberichts, p. 87.
25. *The Admonitions,* no. 6; p. 81, *Omnibus.*
26. *Mirror of Perfection,* Tr. by Leo Sherley-Price, no. 4; p. 1131, *Omnibus.*

Chapter 15.
THE CRÈCHE OF GRECCIO

1. Fortini, p. 564.
2. *Butler's Lives of the Saints*, Volume IV, October 4, "St. Francis of Assisi, Founder of the Friars Minor," p. 28.
3. Fortini, p. 568 (present author's translation).
4. Chalippe, p. 181.
5. *Mirror of Perfection,* no. 6; p. 1132, *Omnibus.*

6. St. Bonaventure, *Major Life*, Chapter 11, no. 1; p. 712, *Omnibus.*
7. *Ibid.*, Chapter 11, no. 2.
8. Celano, *Second Life, Book Two,* Chapter 104, no. 143; pp. 477-478, *Omnibus.*
9. Patriarchal Basilica of St. Mary of the Angels, http://www.porz iuncola.org/english/porziuncolaengli.htm.
10. Traditional Franciscan Life, http://www.franciscan-archive.org/index2.html.
11. St. Bonaventure, *Major Life*, Chapter 10, no. 7; pp. 710-711, *Omnibus.*
12. Celano, *First Life, Book One,* Chapter 30, no. 84; p. 300, *Omnibus.*
13. St. Bonaventure, *Major Life*, Chapter 10, no. 7; pp. 710-711, *Omnibus.*
14. Chalippe, p. 251.
15. "Crib," by Stephen M. Donovan, in *The Catholic Encyclopedia*, Vol. IV, 1908, p. 488, http://www.newadvent.org/cathen/04488c.htm.
16. Fortini, p. 684 (present author's translation).
17. Celano, *First Life, Book One,* Chapter 30, no. 85; p. 300, *Omnibus.*
18. *Ibid.*, no. 86, p. 301.
19. St. Bonaventure, *Major Life*, Chapter 10, no. 7; p. 711, *Omnibus.*
20. Celano, *First Life, Book One,* Chapter 30, no. 86; p. 301, *Omnibus.*

Chapter 16.
SEAL OF THE LIVING GOD

1. St. Bonaventure, *Major Life*, Preface, no. 1; p. 632, *Omnibus.*
2. Dante, *The Divine Comedy: Paradiso*, Canto XI, v. 52-54,http://www.gutenberg.org/etext/8800.
3. *Little Flowers, The Considerations on the Holy Stigmata, The First Consideration*; p. 1432, *Omnibus.*
4. *Ibid., The Second Consideration*; p. 1442, *Omnibus.*
5. St. Bonaventure, *Major Life*, Chapter 8, no. 10; p. 696, *Omnibus.*
6. *Little Flowers, The Second Consideration*; p. 1443, *Omnibus.*
7. Celano, *Second Life, Book Two,* Chapter 127, no. 168; p. 498, *Omnibus.*
8. Pope Pius XI, *Rite Expiatis*, no. 11, http://www.vatican.va/holy_father/pius_xi/encyclicals/documents/hf_pxi_enc_30041926_rite-expiatis_en.html.
9. Celano, *First Life, Book Two,* Chapter 2, no. 93; pp. 307-308, *Omnibus.*
10. *Little Flowers, The Third Consideration*; p. 1448, *Omnibus.*
11. *Ibid.*
12. *Little Flowers, The Fifth Consideration*; p. 1469, *Omnibus.*

13. *Little Flowers, The Third Consideration*; p. 1448, *Omnibus*.
14. Celano, *First Life, Book Two*, Chapter 3, no. 94; p. 309, *Omnibus*.
15. St. Bonaventure, *Excerpts*, no. 10; p. 842, *Omnibus*.
16. St. Bonaventure, *Major Life*, Chapter 13, no. 3; p. 730, *Omnibus*.
17. *Little Flowers, The Third Consideration*; p. 1449, *Omnibus*.
18. *Little Flowers, The Fifth Consideration*; pp. 1468-1469, *Omnibus*.
19. "Mystical Stigmata," by Aug. Poulain, in *The Catholic Encyclopedia*, Vol. XIV, 1912, p. 294, http://www.newadvent.org/cathen/14294b.htm
20. St. Bonaventure, *Major Life*, Chapter 13, no. 3; p. 731, *Omnibus*.
21. *Little Flowers, The Fifth Consideration*; p. 1469, *Omnibus*.
22. *Ibid.*, pp. 1468-1469.
23. Celano, *First Life, Book Two*, Chapter 3, no. 95; p. 310, *Omnibus*.
24. St. Bonaventure, *Major Life*, Chapter 13, no. 4; pp. 731-732, *Omnibus*.
25. *Little Flowers, The Third Consideration*; p. 1451, *Omnibus*.
26. *Ibid.*, p. 1452.

Chapter 17.
GLORIOUS TRANSITUS

1. *Little Flowers, The Third Consideration*; p. 1449, *Omnibus*.
2. *Little Flowers, The Fourth Consideration*; p. 1454, *Omnibus*.
3. *Ibid.*
4. Celano, *Second Life, Book Two*, Chapter 64, no. 98; p. 443, *Omnibus*.
5. *Little Flowers, The Fourth Consideration*; pp. 1455-1456, *Omnibus*.
6. St. Bonaventure, *Major Life*, Chapter 14, no. 2; p. 738, *Omnibus*.
7. *Ibid.*, Chapter 14, no. 1; p. 737.
8. *Ibid.*
9. *Legend of Perugia*, no. 43; p. 1021, *Omnibus*.
10. *Mirror of Perfection*, no. 100; p. 1236, *Omnibus*.
11. *The Writings of St. Francis*, Tr. by Benen Fahy, O.F.M., with Introduction and Notes by Placid Hermann, O.F.M.; p. 128, *Omnibus*.
12. Copyrighted translation from the ancient Italian text by Brother Alexis Bugnolo, editor of The Franciscan Archive, http://www.franciscan-archive.org, used with permission.
13. "St. Francis of Assisi," by Paschal Robinson, in *The Catholic Encyclopedia*, Vol. VI, 1909, p. 221, http://www.newadvent.org/cathen/06221a.htm.
14. Fortini, p. 764.
15. *Mirror of Perfection*, no. 123; p. 1264, *Omnibus*.

16. *Little Flowers, The Fourth Consideration*; p. 1462, *Omnibus.*
17. *Legend of Perugia*, no. 98; p. 1075, *Omnibus.*
18. *Ibid.*, no. 109; pp. 1084-1085.
19. St. Bonaventure, *Major Life*, Chapter 14, nos. 3,4; pp. 738-739, *Omnibus.*
20. *Ibid.*, no. 5; p. 740.
21. *Ibid.*
22. Celano, *First Life, Book Two*, Chapter 8, no. 110; p. 324, *Omnibus.*
23. St. Bonaventure, *Minor Life of St. Francis,* Tr. by Benen Fahy, O.F.M., Chapter 7, no. 6; p. 829, *Omnibus.*
24. *Ibid.*
25. St. Bonaventure, *Major Life*, Chapter 15, no. 4; p. 743, *Omnibus.*
26. *Legend of Perugia*, no. 109; p. 1085, *Omnibus.*
27. "St. Francis of Assisi," by Paschal Robinson, in *The Catholic Encyclopedia*, Vol. VI, 1909, p. 221, http://www.newadvent.org/cathen/06221 a.htm.

Conclusion
ST. FRANCIS AND THE SULTAN

1. John V. Tolan, *Saracens*, pp. 201-202.
2. *Little Flowers*, "Introduction"; p. 1283, *Omnibus.*
3. *Three Companions*, Chapter 7, no. 21; p. 911, Omnibus.
4. Pope Gregory IX, *Mira Circa Nos*, no. 3, http://www.papalencyclicals. net/Greg09/g9mira.htm.
5. Fortini, p. 14.
6. "Muhammad and Saint Francis," by Giulio Basetti-Sani, O.F.M., included in Roy M. Gasnick, Editor, *The Francis Book: 800 Years with the Saint from Assisi,* New York, Macmillan Publishing Company, Inc., 1980, p. 184.

Sources

Print Media

Admonitions, The Tr. by Benen Fahy, O.F.M., Introduction and notes by Placid Hermann, O.F.M., included in *Omnibus*.

A New Fioretti, Tr. by John R. H. Moorman, D.D., included in *Omnibus*.

Anonymous, *St. Francis and the Sultan of Egypt, Thirteenth-Century Testimonies*, Tr. by Paul Oligny, O.F.M., included in *Omnibus*.

Belloc, Hilaire, "The Great and Enduring Heresy of Mohammed," originally from *The Great Heresies*, in *Moslems: Their Beliefs, Practices and Politics*, Ridgefield, CT., Roger A. McCaffrey Publishing, 2002.

Bonaventure, St., *Major Life of St. Francis*, Tr. by Benen Fahy, O.F.M., included in *Omnibus*.

Bonaventure, St., *Minor Life of St. Francis*, Tr. by Benen Fahy, O.F.M., included in *Omnibus*.

Bonaventure, St., *Excerpts from Other Works*, Tr. by Benen Fahy, O.F.M, included in *Omnibus*.

Chalippe, Fr. Candide, O.F.M., *The Life and Legends of Saint Francis of Assisi,* revised and re-edited by Fr. Hilarion Duerk, O.F.M., New York, P.J. Kenedy & Sons, 1918.

Englebert, Omer, and Brown, Raphael, *Chronology*, included in *Omnibus*.

Fortini, Arnaldo, *Nova Vita di San Francesco,* Roma, Carucci Editore, 1981.

Gasnick, Roy M., Editor, *The Francis Book: 800 Years with the Saint from Assisi,* New York, Macmillan Publishing Company, Inc., 1980, p. 184.

Habig, Marion A., Editor, *St. Francis of Assisi: Writings and Early Biographies, English Omnibus of Sources for the Life of St. Francis*, Chicago, Franciscan Herald Press, Third Revised Edition, 1973. Cited herein as *Omnibus*.

Habig, Marion A., O.F.M., *The Franciscan Book of Saints*, Chicago, Franciscan Herald Press, 1959.

Habig, Marion A., O.F.M., and Hegener, Mark, O.F.M., *A Short History of the Third Order,* Chicago, Franciscan Herald Press, Revised Edition, 1977.

Habig, Marion A., O.F.M., *In Journeyings Often,* New York, The Franciscan Institute, 1953.

Hoeberichts, J., *Francis and Islam*, Quincy IL, Franciscan Press, 1997.

Jacques de Vitry, *History of the Orient* (Chapter 32); included in *Omnibus*.

Kedar, Benjamin Z., *Crusade and Mission: European Approaches toward the Muslims*, Princeton, Princeton University Press, 1984.

Legend of Perugia, Introduction, Theophile Desbonnets, Tr. by Paul Oligny, included in *Omnibus*.

Legend of Perugia, Tr. by Paul Oligny, included in *Omnibus*.

Legend of the Three Companions, Tr. by Nesta de Robeck, included in *Omnibus*.

Life of St. Clare Virgin, The, Fra' Tommaso da Celano, Tr. by Catherine Bolton Magrini, Assisi, Editrice Minerva, 2001.

Little Flowers of St. Francis, Tr. by Raphael Brown, included in *Omnibus*.

Maier, Christoph T. , *Preaching the Crusades: Mendicant Friars and the Cross in the Thirteenth Century*, Cambridge, U.K., Cambridge University Press, 1994.

Mirror of Perfection, Tr. by Leo Sherley-Price, included in *Omnibus*.

Powell, James M., *Anatomy of a Crusade, 1213-1221*, Philadelphia, University of Pennsylvania Press, 1986.

Powell, James M., *St. Francis of Assisi's Way of Peace*, manuscript.

Powell, James. M., *"Francesco d'Assisi e la Quinta Crociata, Una Missione di Pace,"* in *Schede Medievali*, 4 (1983).

Roncaglia, Martiniano, *St. Francis of Assisi and the Middle East*, Tr. by Stephen A. Janto, O.F.M., Franciscan Center of Oriental Studies, Cairo, 1954.

Rule of 1221, The, Tr. by Benen Fahy, O.F.M., Introduction and notes by Placid Hermann, O.F.M, included in *Omnibus*.

Rule of 1223, The, Tr. by Benen Fahy, O.F.M., Introduction and notes by Placid Hermann, O.F.M., included in *Omnibus*.

Rule of the Third Order, The, Tr. by Benen Fahy, O.F.M., Introduction and notes by Placid Hermann, O.F.M., included in *Omnibus*.

Spencer, Robert, *The Politically Incorrect Guide to Islam (and the Crusades)*, Washington, D.C., Regnery Publishing, Inc., 2005.

Steck, Francis Borgia, O.F.M., *Glories of the Franciscan Order*, Chicago, Franciscan Herald Press, 1926.

Testament of St. Francis, The, Tr. by Benen Fahy, O.F.M., included in *Omnibus*.

Thomas of Celano, *The First Life of St. Francis, Book One and Book Two*, Tr. by Placid Hermann, O.F.M., included in *Omnibus*.

Thomas of Celano, *The Second Life of St. Francis, Book One and Book Two*,

Tr. by Placid Hermann, O.F.M., included in *Omnibus*.

Thurston, Herbert J., S.J., and Donald Attwater, Editors, *Butler's Lives of the Saints*, Westminster, Maryland, Christian Classics, 1987.

Tolan, John V., *Saracens: Islam in the Medieval European Imagination*, New York, Columbia University Press, 2002.

Trifkovic, Serge, *The Sword of the Prophet,* Boston, Regina Orthodox Press, Inc., 2002.

Writings of St. Francis, The, Tr. by Benen Fahy, O.F.M., with Introduction and Notes by Placid Hermann, O.F.M.; p. 128, *Omnibus*.

Electronic Media

Alighieri, Dante, *The Divine Comedy: Paradiso*, Tr. by Rev. H. F. Cary, M.A., Canto XII, v. 130-132, http://www.gutenberg.org/etext/8800.

"Aziz's Assisi praise for marchers," CNN Web Site, http://www.cnn.com/2003/WORLD/meast/02/15/sprj.irq.aziz.assisi.1330/index.html?eref=sitesearch.

Catholic Encyclopedia, The, New Advent, http://www.newadvent.org/.

Church of S. Francesco in Cannara, The, http://penelope.uchicago.edu/Thayer/E/Gazetteer/Places/Europe/Italy/Umbria/Perugia/Cannara/Cannara/churches/S.Francesco/home.html.

Clare of Assisi, St., *Testament,* translated from the Latin by Brother Alexis Bugnolo, The Franciscan Archive, http://www.franciscan-archive.org/.

Encyclopædia Britannica from Encyclopædia Britannica Premium Service, http://www.britannica.com.

Franciscan Custody of the Holy Land, http://www.christusrex.org/www1/ofm/cust/TShistry.html.

Franciscan Nonviolence, http://www.ofm-jpic.org/peace/nonviolence/nonviolence_en.pdf.

Historical Outline The Secular Franciscan Order, http://www.franciscansfo.org/history2.htm.

Knox, E. L. Skip, *The Fifth Crusade*, Boise State University online course, http://Crusades.boisestate.edu/5th/04.shtml.

Official Portal of St. Anthony of Padua, http://www.saintanthonyofpadua.net/portale/home.asp.

Official Web Site of the Basilica and Sacred Convent of St. Francis in Assisi, http://www.sanfrancescoassisi.org/.

Patriarchal Basilica of St. Mary of the Angels, http://www.porziuncola.org/english/porziuncolaengli.htm.

Pope Gregory IX, *Mira Circa Nos*, no. 3, http://www.papalencyclicals.

net/Greg09/g9mira.htm.

Pope Leo XIII, *Auspicato Concessum*, http://www.vatican.va/holy_father/ leo_xiii/encyclicals/documents/hf_l-xiii_enc_17091882_auspicato-concessum_en.html.

Pope Pius XI, *Rite Expiatis*, http://www.vatican.va/holy_father/pius_ xi/encyclicals/documents/hf_p-xi_enc_30041926_rite-expiatis_en.html.

Rengers, Christopher, O.F.M. Cap,, Capuchin Franciscan Friars, Province of St. Augustine, http://www.capuchin.com/index.php?page=home.

Rule and Form of Life of the Brothers and Sisters of Penance, http:// www.franciscan-sfo.org/Rule1289.htm.

Rule of the Secular Franciscan Order, The, http://www.franciscansfo.org/FFMR/Rule.htm.

Sezzi, Linda, *San Francesco alla corte del sultano. Fallimento del dialogo interreligioso all'alba del XIII secolo?* Thesis, University of Bologna, 2002-2003; http://www.tesionline.com/intl/thesis.jsp?idt=9362.

Story of the Cross, The, http://www.poorclarestmd.org/cross.htm.

Story of the San Damiano Crucifix, The, http://www.monastery icons.com/info/san_damiano_cross.hzml.

Three Translations of The Koran (Al-Qur'an), http://www.gutenberg.org/ files/16955/16955.txt.

Traditional Franciscan Life, http://www.franciscan-archive.org/index2. html.

"The Writings of St. Francis of Assisi," *The Regula Bullata,* Translated from Critical Latin Edition, edited by Fr. Kajetan Esser, O.F.M., by Brother Alexis Bugnolo, Editor of the Franciscan Archive, http://www.fran ciscan-archive.org/patriarcha/opera/rules.html.

About the Author

A third Order (Secular) Franciscan, Frank Rega has long been an avid student of St. Francis of Assisi and of Padre Pio. His first book is entitled *Padre Pio and America*. He moderates a 350-member St. Pio of Pietrelcina internet prayer and discussion group, and hosts a popular Padre Pio web site, www.sanpadrepio.com. A Henry Rutgers Scholar and Phi Beta Kappa member at Rutgers, Mr. Rega studied at Yale University's Institute of Human Relations on a Woodrow Wilson Fellowship. Most recently he was a software consultant for Compuware Corp., assigned to NASA and projects for the Department of Homeland Security.